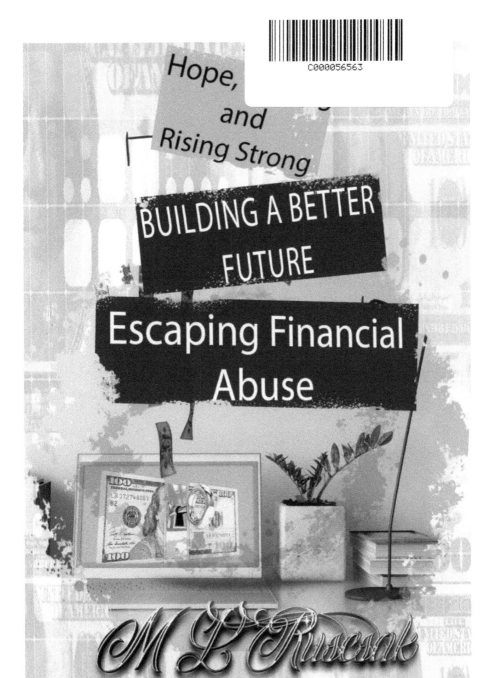

Hope, and Rising Strong

BUILDING A BETTER FUTURE

Escaping Financial Abuse

M L Rusenak

Trient Press
3375 S Rainbow Blvd
#81710, SMB 13135
Las Vegas,NV 89180

Ordering Information:
Quantity sales. Special discounts are available on quantity purchases by corporations, associations, and others. For details, contact the publisher at the address above.
Orders by U.S. trade bookstores and wholesalers. Please contact Trient Press: Tel: (775) 996-3844; or visit www.trientpress.com.

Printed in the United States of America

Publisher's Cataloging-in-Publication data
Ruscsak, M.L.
A title of a book :Working for Your Dreams: Making this year your best year
ISBN
Paperback   979-8-88990-051-1

E-book   979-8-88990-050-4

Building a Better Future: Escaping Financial Abuse

CHAPTER 1 INTRODUCTION

❖   Explanation of financial abuse
❖   Importance of healing from financial abuse
❖   Overview of the book's purpose

Financial abuse is a form of domestic violence that is often overlooked, but can have devastating consequences for survivors. It can take many forms, including restricting access to money, sabotaging credit or job opportunities, and exploiting a partner's financial resources. Financial abuse can have far-reaching effects on a survivor's ability to escape an abusive relationship, build a new life, and achieve financial stability.

Healing from financial abuse is a crucial part of the recovery process for survivors. It involves not only overcoming the practical challenges of rebuilding one's finances, but also addressing the emotional and psychological impact of financial abuse. This book is designed to provide survivors with the tools, resources, and support they need to escape financial abuse and build a better future.

Through personal stories, expert insights, and practical advice, this book aims to shed light on the often-hidden issue of financial abuse, and to help survivors reclaim their power and autonomy. Whether you're currently experiencing financial abuse, have recently left an abusive relationship, or are supporting someone who has, this book is for you. Together, we can build a better future, one that is free from financial abuse and full of hope, healing, and resilience.

Explanation of financial abuse

I never thought that I would be a victim of domestic violence. I was a strong and independent woman, with a good job and a supportive partner. But over time, I began to realize that something wasn't right. My partner was always in control of the money, even though we both worked full-time. He would tell me that he was better with numbers, and that he just wanted to make sure that we were financially stable. At first, I didn't think much of it. But as time went on, I began to feel more and more isolated and trapped.

It wasn't until I started researching financial abuse that I realized what was happening to me. Financial abuse is a form of domestic violence that involves using money as a tool of control. It can take many forms, including:

Controlling access to money: This can include withholding money, limiting access to bank accounts or credit cards, or giving an allowance that is insufficient to cover basic needs.

Sabotaging credit or job opportunities: This can include preventing a partner from obtaining credit, applying for jobs on their behalf without their consent, or sabotaging job interviews or promotions.

Exploiting a partner's financial resources: This can include using a partner's money without their consent, forcing them to take on debt, or pressuring them to sign over assets.

Using financial abuse as a tool of coercion or punishment: This can include threatening to withhold money or ruin a partner's credit, or using financial resources to manipulate a partner into staying in an abusive relationship.

Financial abuse is often closely tied to other forms of abuse, such as physical, emotional, and sexual abuse. For me, the financial abuse was just one piece of a larger pattern of control and manipulation. But it was a powerful piece, and one that made it difficult for me to leave the relationship.

One of the most insidious aspects of financial abuse is that it can be hard to recognize. Money is often a sensitive topic in relationships, and it can be difficult to tell the difference between healthy financial management and abuse. For me, it took a long time to realize that I was being financially abused. I thought that my partner was just trying to help us be financially responsible. But over time, I began to realize that I had no control over our finances, and that I was completely dependent on him for everything.

Financial abuse can have serious consequences for survivors. It can make it difficult to leave an abusive relationship, since the survivor may have limited access to money, credit, or other resources. It can also have long-term effects on a survivor's financial stability, making it harder for them to rebuild their lives after leaving the relationship.

If you think that you may be experiencing financial abuse, it's important to reach out for help. Talk to a trusted friend or family member, or seek out resources from a domestic violence organization. Financial abuse is never okay, and you deserve to be treated with respect and dignity.

In the next chapter, we'll explore the emotional impact of financial abuse, and how survivors can begin to heal and rebuild their lives. Remember, you are not alone, and there is hope for a better future.

Importance of healing from financial abuse

The effects of financial abuse can be long-lasting and far-reaching. When I left my abusive relationship, I was left with no money, no credit, and no sense of financial security. I felt like I had to start my life over from scratch, and the prospect of rebuilding seemed overwhelming. But with time and support, I was able to begin the process of healing from the financial abuse that had kept me trapped for so long.

Healing from financial abuse is important for several reasons. First and foremost, it allows survivors to regain their sense of autonomy and control. When someone is financially abusive, they are essentially taking away their partner's ability to make their own decisions and live their own life. Healing from financial abuse means reclaiming that sense of independence and self-determination.

Healing from financial abuse is also important for survivors' financial stability. Financial abuse can have serious consequences for survivors' credit scores, job prospects, and ability to access resources. Healing from financial abuse means taking steps to rebuild credit, find new job opportunities, and establish a sense of financial security.

But perhaps most importantly, healing from financial abuse is important for survivors' emotional well-being. Financial abuse can be incredibly traumatic, and can lead to feelings of shame, guilt, and worthlessness. It can also make it difficult to trust others and form new relationships. Healing from financial abuse means addressing these emotional wounds and learning to move forward with hope and resilience.

There are many ways to begin the process of healing from financial abuse. One of the most important is to seek out support from others who have gone through similar experiences. This could include joining a support group, talking to a therapist, or connecting with other survivors online. Having a community of people who understand what you've been through can be incredibly validating and empowering.

Another important step is to educate yourself about healthy financial management. For many survivors, financial abuse has left them feeling overwhelmed and helpless when it comes to money. But by learning about budgeting, saving, and investing, survivors can regain a sense of control over their finances and begin to build a more stable future.

Healing from financial abuse also involves addressing the emotional wounds that may have been caused by the abuse. This could include working with a therapist to process trauma, practicing self-care to build resilience, and challenging negative beliefs about oneself that may have been reinforced by the abuse.

For me, healing from financial abuse has been a long and challenging process. But with the support of others and a commitment to my own well-being, I have been able to build a life that is free from abuse and full of hope. If you are a survivor of financial abuse, know that healing is possible, and that you deserve to live a life that is full of joy, freedom, and empowerment.

In the next chapter, we'll explore practical resources and tools that can help survivors of financial abuse build a better future. Remember, you are not alone, and there is hope for a brighter tomorrow.

Overview of the book's purpose

When I first realized that I was experiencing financial abuse, I felt ashamed and alone. I didn't know where to turn for help, and I didn't have anyone to talk to about what I was going through. But as I began to educate myself about financial abuse and connect with other survivors, I realized that I was far from alone. Financial abuse is a widespread problem that affects millions of people every year.

The purpose of this book is to provide survivors of financial abuse with the tools, resources, and support they need to heal and build a better future. Drawing on my own experiences and those of other survivors, this book is designed to be a comprehensive guide to healing from financial abuse.

In the first chapter, we explored the nature of financial abuse and its devastating effects on survivors. In the second chapter, we discussed the importance of healing from financial abuse and the many benefits that can come from taking steps to reclaim one's financial independence and emotional well-being.

In the following chapters, we will delve deeper into specific topics related to healing from financial abuse. These chapters will be written from a survivor's perspective, and will provide practical advice and support for survivors at all stages of the healing process.

Chapter 4 will focus on identifying the signs of financial abuse and taking steps to protect oneself from further harm. We will discuss the various tactics that financial abusers use to control and manipulate their partners, and we will provide practical tips for breaking free from these patterns of abuse.

Chapter 5 will focus on rebuilding one's financial stability after financial abuse. We will discuss strategies for repairing credit, finding new job opportunities, and building a stable financial future. We will also discuss the emotional challenges that come with rebuilding after financial abuse and provide guidance for addressing these issues.

Chapter 6 will focus on the emotional healing process after financial abuse. We will discuss the various emotional wounds that can be caused by financial abuse, including shame, guilt, and self-doubt. We will provide guidance for processing trauma, building resilience, and challenging negative beliefs that may have been reinforced by the abuse.

Chapter 7 will focus on building healthy relationships after financial abuse. We will discuss the challenges that survivors may face when it comes to trust and intimacy, and we will provide guidance for building healthy boundaries and establishing trust with new partners.

Throughout the book, we will also feature survivor stories and uplifting quotes to provide inspiration and support for readers. We believe that healing from financial abuse is possible, and that survivors deserve to live a life that is full of joy, freedom, and empowerment.

We hope that this book will serve as a roadmap for survivors of financial abuse who are seeking to rebuild their lives and create a better future for themselves. We encourage readers to approach this book with an open mind and an open heart, and to know that they are not alone. There is hope, there is healing, and there is a better future waiting for all of us.

CHAPTER 2 THE SURVIVOR'S JOURNEY

- ❖ The survivor's story
- ❖ The emotional impact of financial abuse
- ❖ Moving forward: Steps towards healing

Financial abuse is a devastating form of domestic violence that can have long-lasting effects on survivors. It can happen to anyone, regardless of age, gender, or socioeconomic status. When someone experiences financial abuse, they may feel trapped, helpless, and isolated.

In this chapter, we will explore the survivor's journey after experiencing financial abuse. We will start by sharing survivor stories, to shed light on the realities of financial abuse and the emotional toll it takes. We will then dive into the emotional impact of financial abuse, and discuss some of the common feelings and experiences survivors may have.

Finally, we will discuss steps towards healing and moving forward. We will provide practical tips and strategies for survivors who are looking to rebuild their lives after financial abuse. We will also discuss the importance of seeking professional support, and provide information on resources and organizations that can provide help and guidance.

We hope that this chapter will provide validation and support for survivors of financial abuse. We believe that healing is possible, and that every survivor deserves to live a life that is free from fear, control, and manipulation. We invite you to join us on this journey towards healing and empowerment.

The survivor's story

My journey as a survivor of financial abuse began several years ago, when I met my ex-partner. At first, everything seemed perfect. We fell in love quickly, and he seemed like the perfect partner. He was charming, attentive, and successful, and he always seemed to know exactly what to say to make me feel special.

But as time went on, I began to notice some red flags. He started to control my finances, insisting that he handle all of our bills and expenses. He would get angry if I questioned his decisions, and he started to belittle me for my lack of financial knowledge. He would make me feel guilty for spending money, even on basic necessities like food and clothing.

As time went on, the abuse escalated. He started to use my financial dependence on him as a weapon, threatening to leave me if I didn't do what he wanted. He would manipulate me into doing things that I didn't want to do, using money as leverage. He would also sabotage my efforts to find a job, insisting that I stay home and take care of the house and him. Going as far as using my stay-at-home job as a reason to say I was neglecting him.

It wasn't until I stumbled across an article about financial abuse that I realized what was happening to me. I had never heard of financial abuse before, but as I read more about it, everything started to make sense. I finally had a name for what I was experiencing, and I knew that I needed to get out.

Breaking free from the abuse was one of the hardest things I've ever done. It was scary and overwhelming, and I didn't know if I would be able to make it on my own. But with the help of family and friends, and with the support of local domestic violence resources, I was able to escape.

The journey to healing and empowerment hasn't been easy, but it has been incredibly rewarding. I've learned to stand on my own two feet, both financially and emotionally. I've rebuilt my credit, found a job that I love, and started to save money for my future. I've also worked with a therapist to process the trauma of the abuse, and I've learned to set healthy boundaries and prioritize my own needs and goals.

Through my journey as a survivor, I've learned that healing from financial abuse is possible. It takes time, effort, and support, but it is possible. It's not easy to confront the reality of financial abuse, but it's important to remember that you are not alone. There are resources and support available, and there are others who have been through similar experiences.

If you are experiencing financial abuse, know that you deserve better. You deserve to live a life that is free from manipulation, control, and fear. You have the power to break free from the abuse and build a better future for yourself. It won't be easy, but it will be worth it. You are not alone, and there is hope for healing and empowerment.

"Your story is the key that can unlock someone else's prison. Share your testimony." - Unknown

The emotional impact of financial abuse

Financial abuse can have a profound emotional impact on survivors. It can leave them feeling isolated, ashamed, and powerless. Survivors of financial abuse may also experience a range of emotions such as anger, confusion, and sadness. In this chapter, we will explore the emotional impact of financial abuse, and provide strategies for coping with these feelings.

The Emotional Impact of Financial Abuse

Survivors of financial abuse may experience a range of emotions, including:

Fear: Financial abuse often involves threats or intimidation, which can leave survivors feeling fearful and on edge. They may worry about their safety or the safety of their loved ones.

Shame: Survivors of financial abuse may feel ashamed that they were unable to recognize the abuse or stop it from happening. They may feel embarrassed about their financial situation, and worry about being judged by others.

Guilt: Survivors of financial abuse may feel guilty about the abuse, even though it is not their fault. They may feel responsible for the abuser's behavior, or feel like they could have done something to prevent it.

Anger: Survivors of financial abuse may feel angry at their abuser, or at themselves for allowing the abuse to happen. They may also feel angry at the justice system or society for not doing enough to protect them.

Sadness: Survivors of financial abuse may feel sad about the loss of their financial security, their relationships, and their sense of self. They may also feel grief for the life they thought they had, and the future they envisioned.

Coping Strategies

If you are a survivor of financial abuse, it's important to acknowledge and validate your emotions. Here are some strategies for coping with the emotional impact of financial abuse:

Seek support: Talk to someone you trust about what you're going through. This could be a friend, family member, therapist, or support group. Sharing your story can help you feel less alone and provide validation for your feelings.

Practice self-care: Take care of yourself physically and emotionally. Eat well, exercise, and get enough sleep. Engage in activities that bring you joy and make you feel good.

Challenge negative self-talk: Financial abuse can leave survivors feeling like they are to blame or that they are not good enough. Challenge these negative thoughts with positive affirmations and self-compassion.

Set boundaries: If you are still in contact with your abuser, set clear boundaries around communication and interactions. If necessary, seek a restraining order to protect yourself.

Seek professional help: Consider seeing a therapist or counselor who has experience working with survivors of domestic violence. They can provide guidance and support as you navigate the healing process.

In conclusion, the emotional impact of financial abuse can be significant and long-lasting. However, with time and support, survivors can heal and rebuild their lives. Remember that you are not alone, and there is help available.

"Healing is not about becoming who you were before; it's about realizing who you are

becoming as a result of everything you've been through." - Unknown

Journal Exercises:

Reflect on a time when you felt overwhelmed by your emotions related to your experience with financial abuse. Write about what triggered these emotions and how you coped with them. What could you have done differently?

_____

_____

_____

_____

_____

_____

_____

_____

_____

_____

_____

_____

_____

_____

_____

_____

Write a letter to yourself, acknowledging the strength and resilience you have shown in the face of financial abuse. What qualities have you developed as a result of this experience? What lessons have you learned?

_____

_____

_____

_____

_____

_____

_____

_____

_____

_____

_____

_____

_____

_____

_____

Make a list of people or resources that have been helpful to you in your healing journey. Reflect on why these people or resources have been helpful, and how you can continue to utilize them in your ongoing healing process.

_____

_____

_____

_____

_____

_____

_____

_____

_____

_____

_____

_____

Imagine yourself five years from now, fully healed and free from the emotional impact of financial abuse. What does your life look like?

_____

_____

_____

_____

_____

_____

_____

_____

_____

_____

_____

_____

What steps can you take today to move towards this vision of yourself?

_____

_____

_____

_____

_____

_____

_____

_____

_____

_____

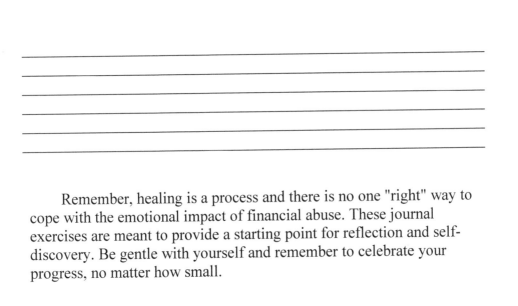

Remember, healing is a process and there is no one "right" way to cope with the emotional impact of financial abuse. These journal exercises are meant to provide a starting point for reflection and self-discovery. Be gentle with yourself and remember to celebrate your progress, no matter how small.

Moving forward: Steps towards healing

It's easy to feel stuck and overwhelmed after experiencing financial abuse. You may be wondering how you can move forward from such a traumatic experience. The truth is, healing is a process and it takes time. But there are steps you can take to begin your journey towards healing and building a better future for yourself.

Acknowledge the Abuse

The first step towards healing is acknowledging that the abuse happened. It's important to recognize that what happened was not your fault and that you did not deserve to be treated that way. Denial can be a common coping mechanism, but it can also delay the healing process. Take time to acknowledge what happened and how it has impacted you.

Journal Exercise: Write a letter to yourself, acknowledging the abuse and how it has impacted you. Be honest about your feelings and allow yourself to feel whatever emotions come up.

_____

_____

_____

_____

_____

_____

_____

_____

_____

_____

_____

_____

_____

_____

Seek Support

You don't have to go through the healing process alone. Seek out support from friends, family members, or a therapist. A support system can provide you with a safe space to process your emotions and offer guidance as you navigate your healing journey.

Journal Exercise: Make a list of people or resources that you can turn to for support. Reflect on why these people or resources are helpful and how you can utilize them in your healing process.

_____

_____

_____

_____

_____

_____

_____

_____

_____

_____

_____

_____

_____

_____

_____

_____

Set Boundaries

Setting healthy boundaries is an important step towards healing from financial abuse. Boundaries can help you regain a sense of control and establish a clear line between what is acceptable and what is not. Setting boundaries can be difficult, especially if you have been conditioned to ignore your own needs and prioritize the needs of the abuser. But remember, you have the right to set boundaries and protect yourself.

Journal Exercise: Reflect on the boundaries you would like to set for yourself. What behaviors are unacceptable?

_____

_____

_____

_____

_____

_____

_____

_____

_____

_____

_____

How can you communicate these boundaries to others?

Practice Self-Care

Self-care is a crucial aspect of the healing process. It can help you manage stress, improve your mood, and increase your resilience. Self-care looks different for everyone, but it can include things like exercise, meditation, spending time in nature, or engaging in creative activities.

Journal Exercise: Make a list of self-care practices that you enjoy or would like to try. Incorporate one of these practices into your daily routine and reflect on how it makes you feel.

_____

_____

_____

_____

_____

_____

_____

_____

_____

_____

_____

_____

_____

Create a Plan for Your Future

Finally, creating a plan for your future can help you regain a sense of purpose and control. This plan doesn't have to be elaborate or set in stone, but it can provide you with a roadmap for moving forward. This can include things like setting financial goals, pursuing education or career opportunities, or focusing on personal growth.

Journal Exercise: Write down your goals for the future. What steps can you take to achieve these goals?

_____

_____

_____

_____

_____

_____

_____

_____

_____

_____

_____
_____
_____
_____
_____

How can you stay motivated and focused?

_____
_____
_____
_____
_____
_____
_____
_____
_____
_____
_____
_____
_____
_____

Remember, healing is a journey, not a destination. It's okay to take things one day at a time and to ask for help when you need it. With time and patience, you can heal from the emotional impact of financial abuse and build a better future for yourself.

"The only way out is through." - Robert Frost

Chapter 3 Breaking the Cycle

- ❖ How to recognize financial abuse
- ❖ Tools for breaking free
- ❖ Overcoming the psychological impact of abuse

Breaking the cycle of financial abuse can be a daunting task, but it is possible. It begins with recognizing the signs of financial abuse and taking action to protect yourself. Once you have identified the abuse, you can take steps towards breaking free and building a better future for yourself.

In this chapter, we will explore the tools and resources available to survivors of financial abuse. We will discuss ways to recognize financial abuse and provide practical advice on how to protect yourself. We will also discuss how to overcome the psychological impact of abuse and move forward towards a brighter future.

Remember, breaking the cycle of financial abuse is not an easy journey, but it is one that is worth taking. By taking the necessary steps to protect yourself and seeking support from others, you can build a better future for yourself and your loved ones.

"Breaking free from financial abuse is not easy, but it is possible. Remember that you are not alone, and that there is help available." - Unknown

How to recognize financial abuse

Financial abuse can be difficult to recognize, as it often happens gradually and can be disguised as concern or care. It is important to understand what financial abuse is and how to recognize it so that you can protect yourself and take action if necessary.

Financial abuse **is a form of domestic violence** that occurs when someone uses money or financial resources to control, manipulate, or exploit their partner. This can include withholding money, controlling access to bank accounts, forcing someone to sign documents, and using credit cards or loans in the other person's name without their permission.

If you are unsure if you are experiencing financial abuse, consider the following questions:

Does your partner control all of the money in the relationship, leaving you with little or no access to funds?
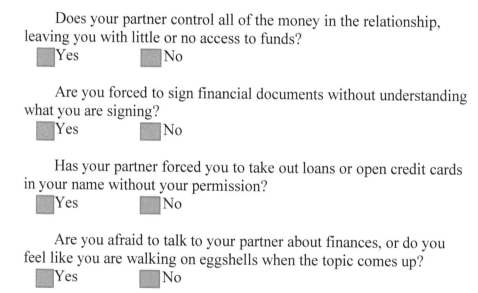 Yes ▢ No

Are you forced to sign financial documents without understanding what you are signing?
▢ Yes ▢ No

Has your partner forced you to take out loans or open credit cards in your name without your permission?
▢ Yes ▢ No

Are you afraid to talk to your partner about finances, or do you feel like you are walking on eggshells when the topic comes up?
▢ Yes ▢ No

Does your partner use money as a way to control or manipulate you, such as threatening to leave you with nothing or using money as a reward for good behavior?

☐ Yes   ☐ No

If you answered yes to any of these questions, it is possible that you are experiencing financial abuse. It is important to reach out for help and support.

Financial abuse is not your fault, and you are not alone. There are resources available to help you escape a financially abusive relationship and take back control of your life. You can reach out to local domestic violence organizations or financial advisors who specialize in helping survivors of financial abuse.

Remember, healing from financial abuse is a journey, and it takes time and effort. But by recognizing the signs of financial abuse and taking steps to protect yourself, you can build a better future for yourself and your loved ones.

"It takes courage to break free from financial abuse, but it's worth it. You deserve to live a life free from fear and control." - Unknown

Tools for breaking free

Breaking free from financial abuse can be a difficult and challenging process, but there are tools and resources available to help you. In this chapter, we will discuss practical steps you can take to break free from financial abuse and begin building a better future for yourself.

Create a safety plan

Before taking any steps towards breaking free from financial abuse, it is important to create a safety plan. This plan should include steps to protect yourself and your children if you have them. Consider contacting a local domestic violence organization for support and assistance in creating a safety plan.

Gather important documents

One of the first steps in breaking free from financial abuse is to gather important documents such as bank statements, credit reports, and legal documents. These documents can be used to establish financial independence and protect yourself in the event of legal proceedings.

Open a separate bank account

Opening a separate bank account is an important step towards financial independence. This account should be in your name only and should not be accessible to your abuser. Consider using a different bank than your abuser to ensure privacy.

Change your passwords

If your abuser has access to your financial accounts, it is important to change your passwords to ensure they no longer have access. Consider using strong, unique passwords that are difficult to guess.

Seek legal assistance

If your abuser has legal control over your finances, it may be necessary to seek legal assistance to regain control. Consider contacting a local legal aid organization or a family law attorney for assistance.

Build a support network

Breaking free from financial abuse can be a difficult journey, but it is important to build a support network to help you through it. Consider reaching out to family, friends, or a support group for survivors of financial abuse.

Remember, breaking free from financial abuse is a process and may take time. Be patient with yourself and take things one step at a time. With the right tools and support, you can break free from financial abuse and build a better future for yourself.

Resources

There are many resources available to help survivors of financial abuse break free and begin building a better future for themselves. Here are a few:

National Domestic Violence Hotline: The National Domestic Violence Hotline provides 24/7 support and assistance to survivors of domestic violence, including financial abuse. They can help you create a safety plan, connect you with local resources, and provide emotional support. You can reach the hotline at 1-800-799-SAFE (7233) or visit their website at www.thehotline.org.

Local domestic violence organizations: Many communities have local organizations that provide support and assistance to survivors of domestic violence, including financial abuse. These organizations may offer counseling, legal assistance, and support groups. You can find loqaqe.

Legal aid organizations: If you need legal assistance to regain control of your finances, there are many legal aid organizations that offer free or low-cost legal services to survivors of domestic violence. You can find legal aid organizations in your area by contacting the National Domestic Violence Hotline or searching online.

Support groups: Connecting with other survivors of financial abuse can be a powerful way to build a support network and begin the healing process. There are many support groups available, both in-person and online. You can find local support groups by contacting local domestic violence organizations or searching online.

Financial resources: There are many financial resources available to help survivors of financial abuse regain control of their finances and build financial independence. These resources may include financial counseling, credit counseling, and assistance with budgeting and saving. You can find financial resources by contacting local domestic violence organizations or searching online.

Remember, breaking free from financial abuse is a journey, and it's important to seek out the support and resources you need to make that journey successfully. Don't hesitate to reach out for help, and know that you are not alone.

"The first step in breaking free from financial abuse is recognizing that it's happening. Once you know what's going on, you can start taking action to regain control of your finances and your life." - Unknown

Journal exercise: Take some time to reflect on your financial situation and any signs of financial abuse that you may be experiencing. Write down your thoughts and feelings, and consider reaching out for help if you need it.

_____

_____

_____

_____

_____

_____

_____

_____

_____

_____

_____

_____

_____

_____

_____

Reflect on what you want your future to look like, and what steps you can take to make that future a reality. Write down your goals and aspirations, and remind yourself that you have the strength and courage to make them happen.

_____

_____

_____

_____

_____

_____

_____

_____

_____

_____

_____

_____

_____

Write down a list of resources and support systems that you can turn to for help as you navigate the process of breaking free from financial abuse. Consider reaching out to a trusted friend, family member, or professional for support.

"You may feel powerless in the face of financial abuse, but you are stronger than you think. Keep fighting for your freedom and your right to a life free from abuse." - Unknown

Journal exercise: Write down a list of things that make you feel empowered and strong. It could be a particular activity, a favorite quote, or a memory of a time when you overcame a challenge. Use these reminders to stay motivated and focused as you work towards breaking free from financial abuse.

_____

_____
_____
_____
_____
_____
_____
_____
_____
_____
_____
_____
_____
_____
_____
_____

Imagine what your ideal life would look like, free from financial abuse and other forms of control. Write down a description of that life, and use it as motivation to keep working towards your goals. Remember that you deserve to live a life that makes you happy and fulfilled.

_____

_____
_____
_____
_____

_____
_____
_____
_____
_____
_____
_____
_____
_____
_____
_____
_____

Overcoming the psychological impact of abuse

"Breaking free from financial abuse is not just about reclaiming your finances - it's about reclaiming your life. You deserve to be happy, healthy, and in control of your own destiny." - Unknown

As survivors of financial abuse, we know all too well the devastating psychological impact it can have on our lives. We may feel overwhelmed, powerless, and trapped in a cycle of abuse that seems impossible to break. But the good news is that there are tools and strategies we can use to overcome the psychological impact of abuse and reclaim our lives. In this chapter, we will explore some of these tools and how to use them effectively.

Seek professional help

One of the most effective ways to overcome the psychological impact of abuse is to seek professional help. A therapist or counselor can provide a safe, supportive space where you can process your experiences, work through your emotions, and develop coping strategies. They can also help you identify any patterns of behavior or thought that may be holding you back and provide guidance on how to move forward.

Practice self-care

Self-care is essential for survivors of abuse. It means taking care of our physical, emotional, and spiritual needs so that we can build resilience and protect ourselves from future harm. Self-care can include activities such as exercise, meditation, spending time in nature, journaling, or engaging in creative pursuits. The important thing is to find what works for you and make it a priority.

Build a support network

Having a support network of friends, family, or other survivors of abuse can be invaluable. It provides a sense of community, validation, and encouragement when we need it most. Reach out to others who understand what you're going through and who can offer empathy and support. Consider joining a support group, attending a workshop or retreat, or connecting with others online.

Set boundaries

Setting boundaries is an essential tool for overcoming the psychological impact of abuse. It means learning to say no to behaviors or situations that are harmful or uncomfortable for us and creating a safe space for ourselves. It can be challenging to set boundaries, especially if we've never done it before, but it's a vital step in reclaiming our power and protecting ourselves from future harm.

Practice forgiveness

Forgiveness is a powerful tool for healing and moving forward from the pain of abuse. It doesn't mean condoning or excusing the behavior of the abuser, but rather, it's a way of releasing the emotional burden that we carry. Forgiveness can help us let go of anger, resentment, and bitterness, and free up space for positive emotions like love, compassion, and joy.

Focus on the present moment

One of the most challenging aspects of overcoming the psychological impact of abuse is letting go of the past and staying present in the moment. We may feel stuck in a cycle of rumination, replaying past events over and over in our minds, or worrying about the future. Practicing mindfulness can help us stay grounded in the present moment, reducing stress and anxiety and promoting feelings of calm and well-being.

By using these tools and strategies, we can break free from the cycle of abuse and reclaim our lives. It's not an easy journey, but with time, patience, and support, we can overcome the psychological impact of abuse and thrive in our new, empowered lives.

In conclusion, breaking the cycle of financial abuse requires recognizing the signs of abuse, building a support system, and addressing the psychological impact of abuse. It's important to remember that healing from financial abuse is a journey, and it's okay to seek help and take things one step at a time. By taking action and seeking resources, survivors can reclaim their power and move towards a brighter future.

Journal exercises:

Reflect on the tools discussed in this chapter for breaking free from financial abuse. Which tools resonate with you the most?

_____
_____
_____
_____
_____
_____
_____
_____
_____
_____
_____
_____
_____

Which ones do you think will be the most challenging to implement in your own life?

_____
_____
_____
_____
_____
_____
_____
_____
_____
_____
_____
_____

_____

_____

_____

_____

Think about a time when you felt trapped or powerless in a
financial situation. What steps did you take to overcome that situation?

_____

_____

_____

_____

_____

_____

_____

_____

_____

_____

_____

_____

_____

How can you apply those lessons to your current situation?

_____

_____

_____

_____

_____

_____

_____

_____

_____

_____

_____

_____

_____

_____

_____

Write a letter to your future self, describing the financial freedom
and empowerment you hope to achieve.

_____

_____

_____

_____

_____

_____

_____

_____

_____

_____

_____

_____

_____

_____

What steps can you take today to move towards that vision?

_____

_____

_____

_____

_____

_____

_____

_____

CHAPTER 4 MOVING FORWARD

❖ Rebuilding self-worth
❖ Developing healthy financial habits
❖ Building a support network

Chapter 4 is all about moving forward and building a new future after experiencing financial abuse. This chapter will explore three key areas that are essential to building a brighter future: rebuilding self-worth, developing healthy financial habits, and building a support network. By focusing on these areas, survivors can not only recover from the trauma of financial abuse, but also create a life filled with financial stability, confidence, and empowerment.

Rebuilding self-worth

Rebuilding Self-Worth

Financial abuse can have a devastating impact on a survivor's self-worth. When someone has been manipulated, controlled, and belittled for their financial decisions, it's easy to begin to doubt their own abilities and worth. Rebuilding self-worth is an essential step towards healing and moving forward.

Recognize the effects of financial abuse on self-worth
One of the first steps towards rebuilding self-worth is recognizing the impact of financial abuse on one's sense of self. It's important to understand that the negative messages received during financial abuse were not true, and that the survivor is capable and deserving of making their own financial decisions.

Challenge negative self-talk

Negative self-talk can be a major obstacle to rebuilding self-worth. It's important to recognize when negative thoughts are taking over and to challenge them with positive affirmations. For example, instead of saying "I'm not good with money," try saying "I'm learning to be more financially literate every day."

Practice self-care

Self-care is essential to rebuilding self-worth. Survivors should focus on taking care of their physical, emotional, and mental health. This can include activities like exercise, mindfulness, therapy, and spending time with supportive friends and family.

Set achievable goals

Setting achievable goals can help rebuild self-worth by providing a sense of accomplishment and progress. Survivors should start by setting small, achievable goals that align with their values and priorities.

Celebrate successes

Celebrating successes, no matter how small, can help boost self-worth and confidence. Survivors should take time to acknowledge and celebrate their accomplishments, no matter how small they may seem.

Journal Exercises

Rebuilding self-worth is a crucial step towards healing from financial abuse. By recognizing the impact of financial abuse on self-worth, challenging negative self-talk, practicing self-care, setting achievable goals, and celebrating successes, survivors can regain their sense of worth and move towards a brighter future.

List Your Strengths: Take some time to reflect on your personal strengths. Write down five things that you are good at, such as your ability to problem-solve or your compassion for others. Reflect on how these strengths have helped you in the past and how you can continue to use them in your life moving forward.

_____
_____
_____
_____
_____
_____
_____
_____
_____
_____
_____
_____
_____
_____
_____
_____
_____
_____

Challenge Your Negative Self-Talk: When we experience financial abuse, it can often impact how we view ourselves. Negative self-talk can keep us from seeing our worth and potential. Write down any negative thoughts or beliefs you have about yourself related to the abuse. Then, challenge each thought with evidence that contradicts it. For example, if you wrote, "I'm not good with money," challenge that thought by writing down times when you made responsible financial decisions.

_____
_____
_____
_____
_____
_____

_____

_____

_____

_____

_____

_____

_____

_____

_____

_____

Write a Letter to Yourself: Imagine you are writing a letter to your future self, five years from now. Write down where you see yourself in your personal and financial life. Be specific about your goals, dreams, and aspirations. This exercise can help you envision a positive future for yourself and set goals to achieve it.

_____

_____

_____

_____

_____

_____

_____

_____

_____

_____

_____

_____

_____

Practice Self-Care: Self-care is an essential part of rebuilding self-worth. Write down five things you can do for yourself each day to promote self-care. It can be as simple as taking a bubble bath or going for a walk. Remember, self-care is not selfish but rather an act of self-love.

_____

_____

_____

_____

_____

_____

_____

_____

_____

_____

_____

_____

_____

_____

_____

Acknowledge Your Accomplishments: Take time to acknowledge your accomplishments, no matter how small they may seem. Write down three things you achieved this week, no matter how small they may seem. Reflect on what you did to achieve them and how they make you feel. Celebrating small victories can help build confidence and self-worth.

Developing healthy financial habits

Developing healthy financial habits after experiencing financial abuse can be challenging, but it is essential for moving forward and building a better future. Here are some steps that can help survivors develop healthy financial habits:

Identify your financial goals: Setting financial goals can help you stay focused and motivated. Ask yourself what you want to achieve financially, whether it's paying off debt, building an emergency fund, or saving for a specific purchase.

Create a budget: A budget is a crucial tool for managing your finances. It allows you to track your income and expenses and helps you stay on top of your financial goals. Create a budget that is realistic and includes all your monthly expenses, such as rent, utilities, groceries, and transportation.

Track your spending: Keep track of your spending to ensure that you are sticking to your budget. This can be done by using a spreadsheet or a budgeting app.

Establish healthy financial habits: Identify unhealthy financial habits that you may have developed as a result of financial abuse and work to replace them with healthy habits. For example, if you have a tendency to overspend, try to limit your discretionary spending and prioritize your financial goals.

Educate yourself: Learn about personal finance and investing to improve your financial literacy. This can help you make informed decisions and feel more confident about your financial future.

Seek professional help: Consider consulting a financial advisor or credit counselor for guidance on managing your finances and improving your credit score.

Developing healthy financial habits can take time and effort, but it is an essential step towards rebuilding your financial independence and achieving your financial goals. Remember to be patient with yourself and celebrate your progress along the way.

Journal Exercises:

What are your financial goals, and why are they important to you?

_____

_____

_____

_____

_____

_____

_____

_____

_____

_____

_____

_____

_____

_____

_____

What are some unhealthy financial habits that you have developed, and how can you replace them with healthy habits?

_____

_____

_____

_____

_____

_____

_____

_____

_____

_____

_____

_____

_____

_____

_____

_____

What steps can you take to improve your financial literacy?

_____

_____

_____

_____

_____

_____

_____

_____

_____

_____

_____

_____

Are there any financial resources or professionals that you could benefit from consulting?

_____

_____

_____

_____

_____

_____

_____

_____

_____

_____

_____

_____

_____

_____

_____

What is one small step that you can take today towards developing healthy financial habits?

_____

_____

_____

_____

_____

_____

_____

_____

_____

_____

_____

_____

_____

_____

Building a support network

Recovering from financial abuse can be a long and difficult journey, but it doesn't have to be a lonely one. One of the most important things you can do for yourself is to build a strong support network. This can include friends, family, support groups, or even a therapist.

It can be challenging to open up and share your experiences with others, especially if you've been conditioned to keep your struggles a secret. However, building a support network can provide a sense of validation, understanding, and connection that is essential for healing. Here are some tips for building a strong support network:

Reach out to trusted friends and family members: Identify the people in your life who you feel safe with and who have your best interests at heart. Be honest with them about what you've been through and how it has affected you. It's okay if you don't feel comfortable sharing everything at once; take things at your own pace.

Join a support group: There are many support groups available for survivors of financial abuse. These groups provide a safe and supportive space to share your experiences, learn from others, and build connections. Look for local groups or online communities that align with your needs and values.

Consider therapy: Therapy can be a valuable tool for healing from financial abuse. A therapist can provide a non-judgmental space for you to process your experiences, explore your emotions, and develop coping strategies. Look for a therapist who specializes in trauma or abuse, and who has experience working with survivors of financial abuse.

Build new relationships: If you've lost touch with friends or family members due to the abuse, or if you feel that your current relationships are not supportive, consider building new relationships.

This can include joining a club or group that aligns with your interests, volunteering, or attending events in your community.

Practice self-care: Taking care of yourself is essential for building a strong support network. Make time for activities that bring you joy and relaxation, such as exercise, hobbies, or meditation. Set boundaries with people who drain your energy or trigger negative emotions, and prioritize your own well-being.

By building a strong support network, you can feel less alone and more empowered in your healing journey. Remember, it's okay to ask for help and support, and to take things at your own pace. With time, patience, and the right resources, you can overcome the impact of financial abuse and build a brighter future for yourself.

Journal Exercises

Who are the people in your life that you feel comfortable talking to about your experiences with financial abuse?

_____

_____

_____

_____

_____

_____

_____

_____

_____

_____

_____

_____

_____

_____

_____

_____

Write down their names and consider how you can deepen those relationships and rely on them more for support.

_____

_____

_____

_____

_____

_____

_____

_____

_____

_____

_____

_____

_____

_____

_____

Are there any support groups or organizations in your community that focus on financial abuse or related issues?

_____

_____

_____

_____

_____

_____

_____

_____

_____

_____

_____

_____

_____

_____

_____

_____

_____

Research these resources and consider attending a meeting or reaching out for support.

_____

_____

_____

_____

_____

_____

_____

_____

_____

_____

_____

_____

_____

Think about the qualities that you value in a friend or support person. Write down a list of these qualities and consider how you can look for these qualities in potential support network members.

_____

_____

_____

_____

_____

_____

_____

_____

_____

_____

_____

_____

_____

_____

_____

Are there any relationships in your life that feel toxic or unsupportive?

_____

_____

_____

_____

_____

_____

_____

_____

_____

_____

_____

_____

_____

_____

Consider how you can set boundaries with these individuals and prioritize relationships that are more positive and uplifting.

Think about any gaps in your support network. Are there areas where you would like more support or connections with others?

_____

_____

_____

Write down some ideas for how you can fill these gaps, such as joining a new social group or reaching out to old friends.

CHAPTER 5 UPLIFTING QUOTES AND STORIES

Quotes from survivors and experts
Personal stories of triumph over financial abuse
Inspirational messages for the reader

Financial abuse can leave survivors feeling isolated and alone. In Chapter 5, we'll share uplifting quotes from survivors and experts, as well as personal stories of triumph over financial abuse. These inspirational messages will serve as a reminder to readers that they are not alone and that healing and a brighter future are possible. Through these stories, readers will see that it's possible to overcome financial abuse and build a better future. So, let's dive in and get inspired!

Quotes from survivors and experts

Quotes from Survivors and Experts

When recovering from financial abuse, it can be incredibly helpful to hear from those who have experienced it before and come out the other side. The following quotes from survivors and experts offer wisdom, guidance, and hope for those who are currently struggling.

"Financial abuse can be so subtle and insidious that it's easy to overlook. But the impact on your life can be devastating. If you suspect you are being financially abused, trust your instincts and seek help." - Leslie, Survivor

"Survivors of financial abuse often blame themselves for their situation, but it's important to remember that abuse is never the victim's fault. You deserve love, respect, and financial security." - Dr. Brené Brown, Research Professor and Author

"Financial abuse is not just about money; it's about power and control. Breaking free from financial abuse means reclaiming your power and taking control of your own life." - Sarah, Survivor

"Recovering from financial abuse takes time and patience, but it's worth it. You can create a life for yourself that is free from abuse and full of possibility." - Dr. Ramani Durvasula, Clinical Psychologist and Author

"Financial abuse can make you feel like you're alone in the world, but you're not. There are people and resources available to help you. You just have to reach out and ask for it." - Maya, Survivor

"Healing from financial abuse means rewriting the story of your life. It means recognizing your own worth and building a future that reflects that worth." - Dr. Sharon Melnick, Business Psychologist and Author

"Financial abuse is a form of domestic violence, and it's just as damaging as physical or emotional abuse. No one deserves to live in fear or to feel trapped. You have the power to break free." - Sarah, Survivor

"Healing from financial abuse requires self-compassion, self-awareness, and self-love. You are worthy of all three." - Dr. Kristin Neff, Associate Professor and Author

"Financial abuse is a tool of oppression, but it's not an unbeatable one. You can take back your power and create a life that is full of joy, abundance, and possibility." - Leslie, Survivor

"Financial abuse can leave you feeling like you have no control over your life, but that's not true. You have the power to create the life you want. It starts with believing in yourself." - Maya, Survivor

These quotes offer a glimpse into the wisdom and strength of survivors and experts who have faced financial abuse and come out the other side. If you're struggling with financial abuse, remember that you are not alone and that healing is possible.

Journal Exercise:
Choose a quote from the list above that resonates with you and write it down. Spend some time reflecting on why this quote speaks to you and how you can apply its wisdom to your own life.

_____

_____
_____
_____
_____
_____
_____
_____
_____
_____
_____
_____
_____
_____
_____
_____

Personal stories of triumph over financial abuse

Personal stories of triumph over financial abuse can be a powerful source of inspiration for those who are currently experiencing financial abuse or have recently escaped it. When survivors share their experiences and stories, it can help others see that they are not alone and that it is possible to overcome the trauma and move forward in a positive direction.

One survivor's story of triumph over financial abuse began when she left her abusive partner with nothing but the clothes on her back and her children in tow. She had no money, no job, and nowhere to go. But she was determined to rebuild her life and provide a safe and secure home for her family.

She started by seeking out resources and support from organizations that specialize in helping survivors of domestic violence and financial abuse. With their help, she was able to find a job and a place to live. She learned how to manage her finances and budget her money so that she could provide for her family and save for the future.

Despite the many challenges she faced, she never gave up. She believed in herself and her ability to create a better life for her family. She surrounded herself with positive, supportive people who encouraged her and helped her to stay focused on her goals.

Over time, she was able to save enough money to buy a small house for her family. She continued to work hard and save, eventually starting her own business and becoming financially independent.

Through her experiences, this survivor learned the importance of seeking out help and support, taking control of her finances, and surrounding herself with positive influences. Her story serves as an inspiration to others who are struggling with financial abuse and shows that it is possible to overcome even the most difficult circumstances.

In addition to personal stories of triumph, there are many uplifting quotes from survivors and experts that can help inspire and motivate those who are healing from financial abuse. Some examples include:

"The greatest weapon against financial abuse is knowledge." - Robyn Spoto, Financial Advocate

"You are not a victim for sharing your story. You are a survivor setting the world on fire with your truth. And you never know who needs your light, your warmth, and raging courage." - Alex Elle, Author and Poet

"Healing takes courage, and we all have courage, even if we have to dig a little to find it." - Tori Amos, Singer and Songwriter

"You have within you right now, everything you need to deal with whatever the world can throw at you." - Brian Tracy, Author and Speaker

These quotes remind survivors that they have the strength and courage within them to overcome financial abuse and rebuild their lives. They also emphasize the importance of seeking out knowledge, support, and healing to help them on their journey.

Journal exercises that can be helpful for survivors in this chapter include reflecting on their own personal stories of triumph and making a list of positive affirmations to help them stay motivated and focused on their goals. They can also write about the people in their lives who have provided them with support and inspiration, and make a plan for building a strong support network moving forward.

Inspirational messages for the reader

As you continue your journey towards healing from financial abuse, it's important to remember that you are not alone. Many survivors have walked this path before you, and have emerged stronger and more resilient as a result. In this chapter, we'll explore some inspirational messages to help you stay motivated and encouraged as you work towards building a better future.

Believe in Yourself

One of the most powerful tools in your journey towards healing is self-belief. When you believe in yourself, you're able to tap into your inner strength and resilience, and overcome even the toughest challenges. Remember that you are capable of achieving great things, and that you deserve to live a life of safety and abundance.

Focus on the Present

While it's important to acknowledge the pain and trauma of your past experiences, it's equally important to focus on the present moment. You have the power to shape your future, and to create a life filled with joy, happiness, and financial stability. By focusing on the present and taking small steps towards your goals every day, you can begin to build the life you deserve.

Embrace Change

Change can be scary, but it can also be a powerful catalyst for growth and transformation. As you work towards healing from financial abuse, it's important to embrace change and to be open to new opportunities and experiences. Remember that every challenge is an opportunity to learn and grow, and that you are capable of overcoming anything that comes your way.

Surround Yourself with Positivity

Negative self-talk and toxic relationships can hold you back from reaching your full potential. Instead, surround yourself with positivity and with people who uplift and inspire you. Seek out supportive friends, family members, or support groups who can offer encouragement, validation, and a listening ear when you need it most.

Celebrate Your Progress

Healing from financial abuse is a journey, and it's important to celebrate your progress along the way. Take time to acknowledge the small victories, and to celebrate the steps you've taken towards building a better future. Whether it's opening a new bank account, creating a budget, or seeking out therapy, every step you take is a step towards greater freedom and independence.

Believe in the Possibilities

As you work towards healing from financial abuse, it's important to keep an open mind and to believe in the possibilities that lie ahead. Remember that your past does not define your future, and that you have the power to create the life you want. Believe in your dreams, and take action every day to make them a reality.

In conclusion, healing from financial abuse is a challenging but rewarding journey. By staying motivated, surrounding yourself with positivity, and embracing change, you can overcome even the toughest obstacles and create the life you deserve. Remember that you are not alone, and that there are many resources and supports available to help you along the way. Keep these inspirational messages in mind as you continue on your journey, and know that you have the power to achieve anything you set your mind to.

"The first step towards getting somewhere is to decide that you are not going to stay where you are." - J.P. Morgan

Journal Exercises:

Reflect on your current situation and write down where you would like to be in the future. What steps do you need to take to get there?

_____

_____

_____

_____

_____

_____

_____

_____

_____

_____

_____

_____

_____

_____

How can you apply the quote above to help you move forward?

_____

_____

_____

_____

_____

_____

_____

_____

_____

_____

_____

_____

_____

_____

_____
_____
_____

Think of a time when you overcame a difficult challenge in your life. What strengths and qualities did you draw upon to get through it?

_____
_____
_____
_____
_____
_____
_____
_____
_____
_____
_____
_____
_____

How can you use those same strengths and qualities to overcome financial abuse and build a better future for yourself?

_____
_____
_____
_____
_____
_____
_____
_____
_____
_____

_____
_____
_____
_____
_____
_____

Write down three things that you are grateful for today. How can you incorporate more gratitude and positivity into your daily life?

_____
_____
_____
_____
_____
_____
_____
_____
_____
_____
_____
_____
_____

How can this help you stay motivated and focused on your goals?

_____
_____
_____
_____
_____
_____
_____
_____

_____

_____

_____

_____

_____

_____

_____

_____

Create a vision board or collage of images that represent your goals and dreams for the future. What steps can you take today to start working towards those goals?

_____

_____

_____

_____

_____

_____

_____

_____

_____

_____

_____

_____

_____

How can you use this visual reminder to stay motivated and inspired on your journey towards healing and recovery?

_____

_____

_____

_____

_____

_____

_____

_____

_____

_____

_____

_____

_____

_____

_____

Take some time to practice self-care and self-compassion. Write down a list of things that bring you joy and make you feel good.

_____

_____

_____

_____

_____

_____

_____

_____

_____

_____

_____

_____

_____

How can you incorporate more of these things into your life?

_____

_____

_____

_____

_____

_____

_____

_____

_____

_____

_____

_____

_____

How can you show yourself love and kindness on a daily basis?

_____

_____

_____

_____

_____

_____

_____

_____

_____

_____

_____

_____

CHAPTER 6 RESOURCES AND SUPPORT

A. Practical resources for survivors
- ➤ Financial counseling services
- ➤ Legal aid clinics
- ➤ Emergency financial assistance programs
- ➤ Job training and placement programs
- ➤ Debt management and credit counseling services
- ➤ Housing assistance programs
- ➤ Community-based resources

B. Information on organizations and support groups
- ➤ National Domestic Violence Hotline
- ➤ National Network to End Domestic Violence
- ➤ National Coalition Against Domestic Violence
- ➤ Women's Law
- ➤ Financial Abuse Survivor Network
- ➤ Local support groups and organizations

C. Helpful tips and advice for building a better future
- ➤ Educate yourself on healthy financial habits
- ➤ Create a safety plan for emergencies
- ➤ Develop a budget and financial plan
- ➤ Build a support network
- ➤ Prioritize self-care and healing
- ➤ Set goals for your future and work towards them
- ➤ Seek out additional resources and support as needed

In addition to the above resources, it's important to note that financial abuse is often closely tied to other forms of abuse, such as physical, emotional, and sexual abuse. Survivors may need to seek out a range of resources and support services in order to fully heal and rebuild their lives. It's important to remember that healing is a journey, and that it's okay to seek out help and support along the way.

Financial abuse can be devastating, but it's important to know that there are resources and support available to help survivors rebuild their lives. This chapter will provide information on practical resources, organizations, and support groups that can help survivors of financial abuse find the help they need to move forward.

Part A: Practical Resources for Survivors

Financial counseling services, legal aid clinics, emergency financial assistance programs, job training and placement programs, debt management and credit counseling services, and housing assistance programs are all available resources for survivors of financial abuse. These resources can provide survivors with the tools and support they need to rebuild their financial stability and move forward in a positive direction.

Part B: Information on Organizations and Support Groups

There are numerous organizations and support groups that can help survivors of financial abuse. The National Domestic Violence Hotline, National Network to End Domestic Violence, National Coalition Against Domestic Violence, Women's Law, Financial Abuse Survivor Network, and local support groups and organizations can all provide resources, information, and support for survivors.

Part C: Helpful Tips and Advice for Building a Better Future

Survivors of financial abuse can take steps to build a better future for themselves. Educating yourself on healthy financial habits, creating a safety plan for emergencies, developing a budget and financial plan, building a support network, prioritizing self-care and healing, setting goals for the future, and seeking out additional resources and support as needed are all important steps in the healing process.

It's important to remember that financial abuse is often interconnected with other forms of abuse, and survivors may need a range of resources and support services in order to fully heal and rebuild their lives. Seeking help and support is not a sign of weakness, but rather a sign of strength and courage. The journey towards healing is a process, and it's important to be kind and patient with yourself along the way.

Remember, you are not alone, and there are resources and support available to help you on your journey towards a brighter future.

A. Practical resources for survivors

Financial counseling services

Financial abuse can have a devastating impact on a survivor's finances, often leaving them with debt, damaged credit, and limited resources to rebuild their lives. Financial counseling services can be an essential tool in helping survivors regain control of their finances and move towards a better future.

Financial counseling services can provide survivors with a range of resources and support, including help with budgeting and financial planning, debt management, credit repair, and accessing financial assistance programs. These services are often provided by trained financial counselors who can work with survivors to develop personalized plans that meet their unique needs and goals.

One of the key benefits of financial counseling services is the ability to help survivors rebuild their credit and finances. Financial counselors can help survivors understand their credit report and identify any errors or inaccuracies that may be negatively impacting their credit score. They can also provide guidance on how to establish good credit habits, such as making on-time payments and keeping credit card balances low.

Financial counseling services can also help survivors access financial assistance programs, such as emergency funds, grants, and low-interest loans. These programs can provide survivors with the financial support they need to cover expenses such as rent, utilities, and food while they work towards a more stable financial future.

In addition to these practical resources, financial counseling services can also provide survivors with emotional support and encouragement. Counselors can help survivors develop a positive mindset and a sense of empowerment, providing them with the tools and resources they need to take control of their finances and build a brighter future.

It's important to note that financial counseling services are often available for free or at a low cost, making them accessible to survivors who may be facing financial hardship. Many organizations, such as non-profits and government agencies, offer financial counseling services to survivors of abuse.

If you are a survivor of financial abuse, reaching out to a financial counselor can be a critical step in your journey towards healing and rebuilding your life. By accessing the resources and support available through financial counseling services, you can regain control of your finances, establish healthy financial habits, and move towards a brighter future.

Legal aid clinics

Legal aid clinics provide crucial support for survivors of financial abuse, helping them navigate the legal system and advocating for their rights. Legal aid clinics offer free or low-cost legal services to individuals who cannot afford private attorneys. These services can include representation in court, legal advice, and assistance with paperwork and documentation.

If you are a survivor of financial abuse, seeking the help of a legal aid clinic can be an important step in breaking free from the cycle of abuse and regaining control over your finances. Here are some things to keep in mind when considering legal aid services:

Know your legal rights: As a survivor of financial abuse, you have legal rights that protect you from further abuse and exploitation. These rights can vary depending on your state and country, so it's important to familiarize yourself with the laws and regulations that apply to your situation. A legal aid clinic can help you understand your legal rights and provide support in enforcing them.

Seek out specialized services: Some legal aid clinics specialize in working with survivors of domestic violence and financial abuse. These organizations often have staff members who are trained to handle sensitive cases and have a deep understanding of the dynamics of abuse. Look for legal aid clinics that have experience working with survivors of financial abuse and have a track record of success in advocating for their clients.

Prepare for your consultation: Before meeting with a legal aid attorney, gather any relevant documentation and information related to your case. This can include bank statements, financial records, police reports, and any correspondence with your abuser. Having this information organized and readily available can help your attorney better understand your situation and provide more effective representation.

Advocate for yourself: Remember that you are the expert on your own experience, and your attorney is there to support you and advocate for your rights. Be honest and open about your situation, and communicate your needs and goals clearly. Ask questions if you don't understand something or if you need more information. You have the right to be treated with respect and dignity throughout the legal process.

Legal aid clinics can provide critical support and advocacy for survivors of financial abuse. If you are in need of legal assistance, don't hesitate to seek out these services and take control of your financial future.

As a survivor of financial abuse, seeking legal aid services can be a daunting and overwhelming process. Here are some journal exercises to help you prepare for and navigate this process:

Write about your legal rights: Take some time to research the legal rights that apply to survivors of financial abuse in your state or country. Write down what you've learned and reflect on how this information makes you feel. Are there any rights that you weren't aware of before? How might this knowledge impact your decision to seek legal assistance?

Reflect on your goals: What are your goals for seeking legal aid services? Are you looking to obtain a protective order, file for divorce, or enforce child support payments? Write down your goals and reflect on how achieving them would impact your life.

Gather information: Take some time to gather any relevant documentation or information related to your case. Write down what you've collected so far and reflect on any additional information you may need. Are there any barriers or challenges to gathering this information? How might you overcome these challenges?

Practice self-advocacy: Write about a time when you advocated for yourself in a difficult situation. How did you feel during the situation? What strategies did you use to advocate for yourself? How can you apply these strategies when working with a legal aid attorney?

Emergency financial assistance programs

Financial abuse can leave survivors feeling trapped and helpless, with limited financial resources and few options for escape. In many cases, survivors may need immediate financial assistance in order to leave an abusive situation and begin rebuilding their lives. Fortunately, there are a number of emergency financial assistance programs available to survivors of financial abuse.

Emergency financial assistance programs are designed to provide temporary financial assistance to individuals and families facing a crisis or emergency situation. These programs can help survivors with a variety of expenses, including housing, utilities, food, and medical bills. Some programs may also provide assistance with transportation, child care, and other expenses related to employment or education.

If you are a survivor of financial abuse in need of emergency financial assistance, there are several programs that may be able to help.

Emergency Assistance Programs

Many states and local governments offer emergency assistance programs to help individuals and families facing a crisis or emergency situation. These programs may provide financial assistance for rent, utilities, food, and other basic needs. Eligibility requirements vary by program, but most programs require proof of income, residency, and the emergency situation.

Temporary Assistance for Needy Families (TANF)

TANF is a federal program that provides temporary financial assistance to low-income families with children. The program is designed to help families become self-sufficient by providing financial assistance, job training, and other support services. Eligibility requirements vary by state, but most states require applicants to have low income, dependent children, and be a U.S. citizen or eligible non-citizen.

Emergency Food Assistance Program (TEFAP)

TEFAP is a federal program that provides emergency food assistance to low-income households. The program provides a variety of food items, including canned goods, cereal, pasta, and other non-perishable items. Eligibility requirements vary by state, but most states require applicants to have low income and be a U.S. citizen or eligible non-citizen.

Women, Infants, and Children (WIC) Program

WIC is a federal program that provides nutrition education, healthy food, and other support services to low-income pregnant women, new mothers, and young children. The program provides food vouchers that can be used to purchase a variety of healthy foods, including fruits and vegetables, whole grains, and dairy products. Eligibility requirements vary by state, but most states require applicants to have low income and be pregnant, breastfeeding, or have a child under the age of five.

The Salvation Army

The Salvation Army is a national organization that provides emergency financial assistance to individuals and families in need. The organization offers a variety of services, including emergency shelter, food assistance, utility assistance, and medical assistance. Eligibility requirements vary by location and service, but most services require proof of income, residency, and the emergency situation.

Non-Profit Organizations

There are a number of non-profit organizations that provide emergency financial assistance to survivors of financial abuse. These organizations may provide assistance with housing, utilities, food, and other basic needs. Eligibility requirements vary by organization, but most require proof of income, residency, and the emergency situation.

If you are in need of emergency financial assistance, it's important to reach out for help as soon as possible. Many programs have limited funding and may have waiting lists, so it's important to apply as soon as you can. Additionally, some programs may require documentation or other proof of the emergency situation, so it's important to gather any necessary documents before applying.

Journal Exercises:

Take some time to research the emergency financial assistance programs in your area. Write down the names of the programs and their contact information.

_____

_____

_____

_____

_____

_____

_____

_____

_____

_____

_____

_____

_____

_____

_____

_____

_____

Think about the types of expenses you might need help with in an emergency situation.

_____

_____

_____

_____

_____

_____

_____

_____

_____

_____

_____

_____

_____

_____

Job training and placement programs

Of the many challenges that survivors of financial abuse face, one of the most daunting is finding stable employment. For many survivors, their abuser may have prevented them from working or sabotaged their job prospects, leaving them without the skills or experience necessary to find and maintain gainful employment. Fortunately, there are a number of job training and placement programs available that can help survivors build their skills, connect with potential employers, and take the first steps towards financial independence.

Job training programs can vary widely in terms of their scope and approach, but many focus on providing hands-on training and real-world experience in a particular industry or field. Some programs may offer classroom instruction, while others may prioritize apprenticeships, internships, or other forms of on-the-job training. The goal of these programs is to provide survivors with the skills and knowledge they need to succeed in a particular job or career path.

Placement programs, on the other hand, focus on helping survivors find and secure employment once they have completed their training. These programs may offer assistance with resume building, job search strategies, and interview skills, as well as networking opportunities and job referrals. By connecting survivors with potential employers and helping them navigate the often complex job market, these programs can be an invaluable resource for survivors seeking to rebuild their lives and achieve financial stability.

While job training and placement programs can be incredibly helpful for survivors of financial abuse, it's important to note that they are not a one-size-fits-all solution. Different programs may be better suited to different individuals depending on their interests, skills, and experience, and it's important to do your research and find a program that is a good fit for you. Additionally, some programs may have specific eligibility requirements, such as age, income, or education level, so be sure to carefully review the program's criteria before applying.

If you are interested in exploring job training and placement programs as a survivor of financial abuse, there are a number of resources available to help you get started. Some good places to start include:

Your local Department of Labor or Employment Services office: Many state and local governments offer job training and placement programs, and your local employment services office can help you connect with these resources.

Nonprofit organizations: There are a number of national and local nonprofits that focus on providing job training and placement services to underserved populations, including survivors of abuse. Some examples include Dress for Success, which provides professional attire and job training to women, and Goodwill Industries, which offers a range of job training and placement services.

Community colleges and vocational schools: Many community colleges and vocational schools offer certificate and degree programs in a variety of fields, from healthcare and technology to construction and trades. These programs can be an excellent way to gain new skills and connect with potential employers.

Online resources: There are a number of online resources available to help you find job training and placement programs in your area, including websites like CareerOneStop and MyNextMove.

While job training and placement programs can be an excellent resource for survivors of financial abuse, it's important to remember that they are just one piece of the puzzle. Rebuilding after financial abuse takes time, patience, and perseverance, and it's important to prioritize self-care, healing, and ongoing support as you work towards your goals. With the right resources and a strong support network, however, it is possible to overcome the challenges of financial abuse and build a brighter future.

Debt management and credit counseling services

Dealing with financial abuse often leaves survivors with overwhelming debt and credit problems. The abuser may have opened credit accounts in the survivor's name, used joint accounts irresponsibly, or ruined the survivor's credit score by not paying bills. In many cases, survivors find themselves facing bankruptcy or being sued by creditors for debts they didn't even know they had.

If you're a survivor dealing with debt and credit problems, know that you're not alone. Many organizations offer debt management and credit counseling services to help you get back on your feet. These services can help you create a plan to pay off your debts, negotiate with creditors, and rebuild your credit score.

What Are Debt Management and Credit Counseling Services?

Debt management and credit counseling services are designed to help people who are struggling with debt and credit problems. These services typically offer:

Credit counseling: Credit counselors can help you review your credit report, understand your credit score, and develop a plan to improve it.

Budgeting advice: Counselors can help you create a budget that works for your income and expenses, and identify areas where you can cut back.

Debt management plans: Debt management plans allow you to consolidate your debts into one monthly payment, which is then distributed to your creditors. These plans typically involve reduced interest rates and fees.

Negotiation with creditors: Credit counselors can negotiate with your creditors to reduce interest rates, waive fees, or arrange for a repayment plan that works for you.

Debt management and credit counseling services can be a great way to get a handle on your debt and credit problems. However, it's important to choose a reputable organization and be wary of scams. Look for organizations that are accredited by the National Foundation for Credit Counseling (NFCC) or the Financial Counseling Association of America (FCAA).

How Can Debt Management and Credit Counseling Services Help Survivors of Financial Abuse?

Dealing with the aftermath of financial abuse can be a daunting task, especially when it comes to debt and credit problems. However, debt management and credit counseling services can be an invaluable resource for survivors. Here are some ways these services can help:

Create a plan to pay off debt: Debt management plans can help you pay off your debts in a structured way, making it easier to manage your payments and avoid falling further into debt. Counselors can help you develop a realistic plan based on your income, expenses, and debt load.

Negotiate with creditors: Credit counselors can negotiate with your creditors on your behalf, helping you reduce interest rates and fees, and work out a repayment plan that fits your budget. This can help you avoid bankruptcy or other drastic measures.

Rebuild your credit: Many debt management and credit counseling services offer credit counseling, which can help you understand your credit report and develop a plan to improve your credit score. Counselors can also help you dispute errors on your credit report and avoid making common credit mistakes.

Provide emotional support: Survivors of financial abuse may feel overwhelmed, anxious, or ashamed about their debt and credit problems. Debt management and credit counseling services can provide emotional support, helping survivors feel more confident and in control of their financial situation.

Tips for Working with Debt Management and Credit Counseling Services

Here are some tips to help you get the most out of debt management and credit counseling services:

Do your research: Make sure to choose a reputable organization that is accredited by the NFCC or FCAA. Check the organization's ratings and reviews, and ask for references if possible.

Be honest and transparent: In order for debt management and credit counseling services to be effective, you must be completely honest about your financial situation. This includes being transparent about your income, expenses, and debts. Your counselor can only provide tailored advice and solutions if they have a full understanding of your financial picture.

Create a realistic budget: Your counselor will help you create a budget that takes into account all of your expenses, debts, and income. It's important to be realistic about what you can afford to pay each month, and to stick to the budget as closely as possible.

Explore all options: Debt management and credit counseling services may not be the best solution for everyone. Your counselor should be able to provide information on alternative options, such as debt settlement or bankruptcy. It's important to weigh the pros and cons of each option before making a decision.

Stay committed: Debt management and credit counseling services require a commitment to making consistent payments and following a strict budget. It may take time and discipline, but the end result can be a debt-free future and improved financial stability.

Don't be afraid to ask questions: If you don't understand something, or if you need clarification, don't be afraid to ask your counselor. It's important to have a clear understanding of the process and what is expected of you.

Remember that debt management and credit counseling services are not a quick fix, but rather a long-term solution for improving your financial situation. With commitment and dedication, you can work towards a debt-free future and a brighter financial outlook.

As a survivor of financial abuse, seeking out debt management and credit counseling services can be a daunting task. It may feel overwhelming to confront the extent of the debt and the challenges it poses. However, taking this step can be a crucial component of regaining financial control and stability.

When I first reached out for debt management and credit counseling services, I was filled with a mix of hope and anxiety. I was hopeful that I could finally get a handle on my debt and start to rebuild my financial future, but I was also anxious about what the process would entail and whether or not I would be successful.

Fortunately, I found a reputable and supportive organization that provided me with the guidance and resources I needed to start making progress. My counselor was patient and understanding, and worked with me to create a realistic budget and debt repayment plan. While it was challenging at times, I remained committed to the process and was able to successfully pay off my debts.

Looking back, I am so grateful that I took the step to seek out debt management and credit counseling services. It was a crucial part of my journey towards financial stability and empowerment. If you are a survivor of financial abuse and are struggling with debt, I encourage you to consider reaching out for help. It may be the first step towards a brighter financial future.

Housing assistance programs

If you're a survivor of financial abuse, finding and maintaining safe and stable housing can be one of the biggest challenges you face. Housing assistance programs can provide you with the support you need to get back on your feet and build a brighter future.

Types of Housing Assistance Programs

There are a variety of housing assistance programs available to survivors of financial abuse, including:

Emergency Shelter Programs: These programs provide immediate, short-term housing and support services for individuals and families who are fleeing abuse or are homeless. Emergency shelter programs typically offer safe and secure housing, meals, and basic necessities such as clothing and toiletries. They may also offer counseling, advocacy, and referrals to other services.

Transitional Housing Programs: Transitional housing programs provide longer-term housing and support services for survivors who are working towards self-sufficiency. These programs typically offer affordable housing, as well as support services such as counseling, job training, and financial management.

Rental Assistance Programs: Rental assistance programs provide financial assistance to help low-income individuals and families pay for housing. These programs can help you pay for rent, utilities, and other housing-related expenses, and may also offer support services such as counseling and referrals to other resources.

Homeownership Programs: Homeownership programs can help you achieve your dream of owning a home. These programs offer financial assistance, such as down payment and closing cost assistance, as well as education and counseling to help you prepare for homeownership.

Benefits of Housing Assistance Programs

Housing assistance programs offer a variety of benefits to survivors of financial abuse, including:

Safe and stable housing: Housing assistance programs provide survivors with safe and stable housing, which is critical for their physical and emotional well-being.

Support services: Housing assistance programs often offer support services such as counseling, job training, and financial management. These services can help survivors build the skills they need to become self-sufficient and achieve their goals.

Financial assistance: Many housing assistance programs provide financial assistance to help survivors pay for housing-related expenses, such as rent and utilities.

Referrals to other resources: Housing assistance programs can connect survivors with other resources and services, such as legal aid, healthcare, and childcare.

How to Access Housing Assistance Programs

To access housing assistance programs, you will need to research the options available in your area and determine which programs you are eligible for. Here are some steps you can take to get started:

Contact your local domestic violence organization: Your local domestic violence organization can provide you with information on housing assistance programs and other resources that may be available to you.

Contact your local housing authority: Your local housing authority can provide you with information on rental assistance programs and other housing-related resources.

Research homeownership programs: If you are interested in homeownership, research homeownership programs in your area and determine whether you are eligible to participate.

Apply for assistance: Once you have identified the programs you are interested in, follow the application process to apply for assistance.

Tips for Making the Most of Housing Assistance Programs

Here are some tips to help you make the most of housing assistance programs:

Be honest and transparent: When working with housing assistance programs, it's important to be honest and transparent about your situation and your needs. This will help the program staff provide you with the best possible support.

Follow the rules: Housing assistance programs often have specific rules and requirements that participants must follow. Make sure you understand these rules and follow them in order to maintain your housing assistance.

Participate in support services: Many housing assistance programs offer support services such as counseling and job training. Participating in these services can help you build the skills you need to become self-sufficient and achieve your goals.

Be patient: Housing assistance programs can be competitive, and it may take time to secure a spot in a program or find suitable housing. Be patient and persistent in your search, and don't give up hope.

Stay committed: Once you have secured housing assistance, it's important to stay committed to the program and to your goals. This may mean attending regular meetings or check-ins, participating in support services, and following the program rules.

Celebrate your progress: Celebrate your successes along the way, no matter how small they may seem. Every step forward is a step towards building a better future for yourself and your loved ones.

It's important to note that housing assistance programs may have specific eligibility requirements, such as income limits or residency requirements. Make sure to do your research and check with program staff to determine if you are eligible for assistance.

In addition to housing assistance programs, there are other resources available for survivors of financial abuse who are experiencing homelessness or housing instability. Local homeless shelters and housing organizations may be able to provide temporary shelter and support services. It's also important to reach out to community resources, such as food banks and public assistance programs, for additional support.

Remember, financial abuse and homelessness are not your fault, and there is help available to support you in rebuilding your life. Don't be afraid to reach out for help and support, and stay committed to your journey towards financial stability and independence.

Community-based resources

Community-based resources can be a vital source of support for survivors of financial abuse. These resources can range from community centers and local non-profits to faith-based organizations and social clubs. Community-based resources can provide survivors with a sense of belonging, connection, and support that can be invaluable during the healing and recovery process.

One of the key benefits of community-based resources is that they are often free or low-cost, making them accessible to individuals who may not have the financial resources to pay for expensive services. Community-based resources can provide a wide range of services, including counseling, support groups, job training, legal aid, and financial assistance. Many community-based resources also offer educational programs and workshops on topics such as budgeting, credit management, and financial planning.

One of the best ways to find community-based resources in your area is to start by reaching out to local community centers and non-profits. These organizations often have a wealth of resources and connections that can be invaluable for survivors of financial abuse. Local religious institutions and social clubs can also be a great source of support, providing a sense of community and connection that can be especially important for survivors who may feel isolated or alone.

When seeking out community-based resources, it's important to keep in mind that not all resources may be a good fit for your specific needs and situation. It's important to do your research and ask questions to ensure that you are accessing the right resources for your needs. Be sure to ask about the services provided, the qualifications of the staff, and any fees or costs associated with the services.

One of the benefits of community-based resources is that they often provide a safe and supportive environment where survivors can connect with others who have shared experiences. Many community-based resources offer support groups where survivors can come together to share their experiences, offer support, and find a sense of community. These groups can be especially helpful for survivors who may feel isolated or alone, providing a sense of connection and validation that can be invaluable during the healing process.

In addition to support groups, many community-based resources also offer counseling services that can help survivors navigate the emotional and psychological impact of financial abuse. Counseling can be an important part of the healing process, providing survivors with a safe and confidential space to process their experiences, explore their feelings, and work towards healing and recovery.

Another important resource provided by community-based organizations is job training and placement programs. These programs can help survivors gain the skills and confidence they need to re-enter the workforce and become self-sufficient. Job training programs can provide survivors with training and education in fields such as healthcare, technology, and construction, while job placement programs can help survivors connect with employers who are looking for skilled and motivated workers.

Community-based resources can also provide survivors with access to legal aid and advocacy services. These services can be invaluable for survivors who are seeking legal protection or assistance in navigating complex legal issues related to financial abuse. Legal aid services can provide survivors with advice and representation in areas such as divorce, child custody, and restraining orders, while advocacy services can help survivors navigate the criminal justice system and connect with other resources and support services.

In conclusion, community-based resources can be a vital source of support for survivors of financial abuse. These resources can provide survivors with a sense of belonging, connection, and support that can be invaluable during the healing and recovery process. When seeking out community-based resources, it's important to do your research, ask questions, and choose resources that are the right fit for your specific needs and situation. Remember that healing is a journey, and that accessing the right resources and support services can be a crucial part of that journey.

B. Information on organizations and support groups

National Domestic Violence Hotline

The National Domestic Violence Hotline (NDVH) is a crucial resource for survivors of domestic violence, including those who have experienced financial abuse. Founded in 1996, the NDVH provides 24/7 support, information, and referrals to survivors of domestic violence and their loved ones. The hotline is available in both English and Spanish and can be reached by phone, text, or chat.

If you are experiencing financial abuse, reaching out to the NDVH can be a helpful first step towards getting the support and resources you need. The trained advocates at the NDVH can provide you with information about financial abuse and help you develop a safety plan to protect yourself and your assets. They can also refer you to local resources such as shelters, legal aid clinics, and financial counseling services.

One of the benefits of reaching out to the NDVH is the ability to speak with someone who is trained to understand the unique challenges faced by survivors of domestic violence. The advocates at the NDVH are knowledgeable about the dynamics of abuse, including financial abuse, and can provide non-judgmental support and guidance.

If you are considering reaching out to the NDVH, it can be helpful to prepare in advance. You may want to think about what information you would like to share with the advocate, such as the type of abuse you are experiencing and your current safety concerns. You may also want to consider what resources or support you are looking for, such as legal assistance or financial counseling.

Remember, it is okay to reach out for help and support. The NDVH is here to provide a safe and confidential space for survivors of domestic violence to share their experiences and get the help they need.

Journal Exercise:

If you are considering reaching out to the National Domestic Violence Hotline, take some time to reflect on your reasons for doing so. What specific support or resources are you hoping to receive?

_____

_____

_____

_____

_____

_____

_____

_____

_____

_____

_____

_____

_____

What concerns or fears do you have about reaching out?

Write down your thoughts and feelings in a journal, and consider discussing them with a trusted friend or family member. Remember, reaching out for help is a courageous and important step towards healing and building a better future.

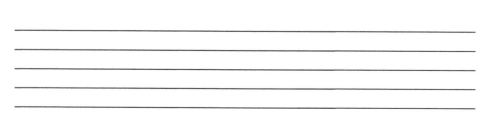

National Network to End Domestic Violence

National Network to End Domestic Violence (NNEDV) is a national organization that works to end domestic violence and empower survivors. Founded in 1990, NNEDV has been at the forefront of the movement to end domestic violence for over three decades. In this chapter, we'll explore the services and resources offered by NNEDV and how they can help survivors of domestic violence.

Services and Resources Offered by NNEDV

NNEDV offers a wide range of services and resources to support survivors of domestic violence. Here are just a few of the ways that NNEDV can help:

Advocacy and Policy: NNEDV advocates for policies and laws that protect survivors of domestic violence and hold abusers accountable. They work with lawmakers at the national, state, and local levels to promote legislation that supports survivors and addresses the root causes of domestic violence.

Training and Technical Assistance: NNEDV provides training and technical assistance to advocates, service providers, and others who work with survivors of domestic violence. Their training programs cover a range of topics, including legal advocacy, economic empowerment, and digital privacy and safety.

Awareness and Education: NNEDV works to raise awareness about domestic violence and educate the public about the issues surrounding it. They offer resources and tools for individuals and organizations to help them take action and promote change in their communities.

Support for Survivors: NNEDV provides support and resources for survivors of domestic violence, including a national helpline and online chat service. They also offer information and referrals to local service providers and organizations that can provide additional support.

How NNEDV Can Help Survivors

If you are a survivor of domestic violence, NNEDV can be an invaluable resource for support and assistance. Here are a few of the ways that NNEDV can help:

Connect you with local resources: NNEDV can provide referrals to local service providers and organizations that can help you with your specific needs. Whether you need emergency shelter, legal assistance, or counseling, NNEDV can connect you with the resources you need.

Provide emotional support: NNEDV's national helpline and online chat service offer confidential emotional support for survivors of domestic violence. They can provide a listening ear, offer advice, and connect you with additional resources as needed.

Offer information and education: NNEDV offers a wealth of information and resources on their website, including information on legal rights, safety planning, and self-care. They also offer webinars, training programs, and other educational resources to help survivors and advocates stay informed and up-to-date on the issues surrounding domestic violence.

Advocate for your rights: NNEDV advocates for policies and laws that protect the rights of survivors of domestic violence. They work with lawmakers and policy makers to ensure that survivors have access to the resources and support they need to heal and rebuild their lives.

If you are a survivor of domestic violence, it's important to know that you are not alone. NNEDV and other organizations are here to support you and help you navigate the challenges you may be facing.

Tips for Getting the Most out of NNEDV's Services

Here are a few tips to help you get the most out of NNEDV's services:

Reach out for help: If you are in need of support, don't hesitate to reach out to NNEDV's national helpline or online chat service. They are available 24/7 and can provide confidential support and assistance.

Take advantage of training and education opportunities: NNEDV offers a range of training and education programs that can help you build your skills and knowledge. Whether you're a survivor or an advocate, these programs can help you stay informed and empowered.

Get involved: NNEDV offers a variety of ways to get involved, from volunteering to advocacy work. Participating in these activities can help you connect with others who share your experiences and passions, and can provide a sense of purpose and fulfillment.

Advocate for change: NNEDV is committed to ending domestic violence and advocating for policies and programs that support survivors. You can help make a difference by speaking out about your experiences and advocating for change in your community and beyond.

Prioritize self-care: Survivors of domestic violence often experience trauma and may struggle with mental health issues. It's important to prioritize self-care and seek out resources and support that can help you heal and recover.

Remember that healing is a journey: Healing from the trauma of domestic violence can take time, and there may be ups and downs along the way. Remember that it's okay to seek out help and support as needed, and that healing is a journey, not a destination.

In conclusion, the National Network to End Domestic Violence is a valuable resource for survivors of domestic violence and their advocates. Whether you are in need of support, education, or advocacy, NNEDV offers a wide range of services and programs to meet your needs. By reaching out for help, getting involved, and advocating for change, you can help create a world free from domestic violence and build a brighter future for yourself and others.

National Coalition Against Domestic Violence

The National Coalition Against Domestic Violence (NCADV) is a national organization dedicated to ending domestic violence and supporting survivors. Their mission is to create a culture where domestic violence is not tolerated, and where all survivors have access to the resources and support they need to heal and rebuild their lives. If you are a survivor of domestic violence, NCADV can be a valuable resource in your journey to healing and recovery.

Here are some tips to help you get the most out of NCADV's services:

Take advantage of their resources: NCADV offers a variety of resources for survivors, including information on safety planning, legal rights, and financial assistance. They also provide a directory of local resources that can help you find support in your community. Take advantage of these resources to get the help and support you need.

Connect with other survivors: NCADV offers a survivors network that connects survivors with each other for support and advocacy. This network can be a valuable source of encouragement and inspiration as you work to heal and rebuild your life.

Advocate for change: NCADV is dedicated to creating systemic change to end domestic violence. You can get involved in their advocacy efforts by contacting your elected officials, participating in awareness campaigns, and supporting policy initiatives that aim to prevent domestic violence and support survivors.

Be patient with yourself: Healing from domestic violence is a journey, and it can take time. Be patient with yourself and give yourself the time and space you need to heal and recover. Remember that you are not alone, and that there are resources and support available to help you along the way.

If you are in immediate danger, call 911 or your local emergency services. If you need support, call the National Domestic Violence Hotline at 1-800-799-7233 or visit their website at www.thehotline.org. They are available 24/7 to provide support and assistance.

Women's Law

As a survivor of domestic violence, it can be difficult to navigate the legal system on your own. Thankfully, there are resources available to help you understand your rights and get the legal support you need. Women's Law is one such resource that provides legal information and support to survivors of domestic violence, sexual assault, and other forms of gender-based violence.

Here are some tips to help you get the most out of Women's Law:

Use the Legal Information and Resources on Women's Law's Website

Women's Law offers a wealth of legal information and resources on their website. This includes state-specific legal information on domestic violence, custody, immigration, and other legal issues that may be relevant to survivors. The website also has a hotline directory that can help you find local resources and support.

Consider Using Women's Law's Email Hotline

If you have a legal question or concern, Women's Law's email hotline can be a valuable resource. You can send an email to their legal team, and they will provide you with legal information and support. The email hotline is confidential and free.

Participate in Women's Law's Webinars and Trainings

Women's Law offers webinars and trainings on a variety of legal topics related to domestic violence and other forms of gender-based violence. These trainings can help you understand your legal rights and build the skills you need to advocate for yourself. You can participate in these trainings from the comfort of your own home, and many of them are free.

Get Involved with Women's Law's Advocacy Efforts
Women's Law is also involved in advocacy efforts to promote policies that support survivors of domestic violence and other forms of gender-based violence. You can get involved with their advocacy efforts by signing up for their newsletter, following them on social media, and participating in their campaigns.

Reach Out for Direct Legal Support

In addition to providing legal information and resources, Women's Law also offers direct legal support to survivors of domestic violence. They have a network of pro bono attorneys who can provide legal representation to survivors in certain circumstances. You can contact their legal team for more information about this program.

Remember, as a survivor, you have the right to legal support and resources. Women's Law is just one of the many resources available to you. Don't hesitate to reach out for the help you need to navigate the legal system and protect your rights.

Financial Abuse Survivor Network

Financial abuse is a devastating form of domestic violence that can leave survivors feeling trapped and powerless. Financial abuse can take many forms, including restricting access to money, controlling spending, and stealing or destroying property. If you are a survivor of financial abuse, it's important to know that you are not alone. There are resources available to help you rebuild your financial independence and take control of your life.

One such resource is the Financial Abuse Survivor Network (FASN). FASN is a non-profit organization dedicated to empowering survivors of financial abuse through education, support, and advocacy. Here are some tips to help you get the most out of FASN's services:

Reach out for help: If you are in need of support, don't hesitate to reach out to FASN. They offer a range of resources and services, including a 24/7 helpline and online support groups.

Get educated: FASN offers a range of educational resources to help survivors understand their rights and options. These resources can help you build your financial knowledge and empower you to make informed decisions about your finances.

Take advantage of support services: FASN offers a range of support services, including financial coaching and counseling. These services can help you develop a plan to rebuild your financial independence and achieve your goals.

Be patient: Recovering from financial abuse can be a long and difficult process. It's important to be patient with yourself and to celebrate small victories along the way.

Here are some additional tips to help you rebuild your financial independence after experiencing financial abuse:

Create a safety plan: If you are still in a relationship with your abuser, it's important to create a safety plan to protect yourself and your finances. This may include opening a separate bank account, changing your passwords, and setting up a PO box for important mail.

Gather important documents: Make sure to gather important financial documents such as bank statements, tax returns, and insurance policies. These documents can help you build a clear picture of your finances and ensure that you have access to important information.

Set financial goals: Setting financial goals can help you stay focused and motivated as you work to rebuild your financial independence. Whether your goal is to pay off debt, save for a down payment on a house, or start a business, having a clear goal in mind can help you stay on track.

Create a budget: Creating a budget can help you manage your finances and ensure that you are living within your means. Make sure to include all of your expenses, including rent, utilities, groceries, and any debt payments.

Build your credit: Building your credit is an important part of rebuilding your financial independence. Make sure to check your credit report regularly and work to improve your score by making on-time payments and keeping your credit utilization low.

Consider seeking legal assistance: If you are dealing with legal issues related to your finances, such as divorce or bankruptcy, it may be helpful to seek the assistance of a lawyer who specializes in these areas.

Remember, rebuilding your financial independence after experiencing financial abuse is a process. It's important to be patient and to seek out support as you work to achieve your goals. With the help of organizations like FASN and a strong support network, you can take control of your finances and your life.

Local support groups and organizations

As a survivor of domestic violence, it can be incredibly isolating and overwhelming to try to navigate the road to healing and recovery on your own. That's why it's so important to reach out for support and connect with local organizations and support groups that can help you along the way.

Here are a few tips to help you get the most out of local support groups and organizations:

Research your options: Take the time to research the different organizations and support groups available in your area. Look for groups that specialize in domestic violence and that have a strong reputation in your community.

Connect with other survivors: One of the most powerful aspects of local support groups is the opportunity to connect with other survivors who understand what you're going through. Building connections with other survivors can help you feel less alone and provide you with a sense of community.

Attend meetings regularly: Consistency is key when it comes to attending support group meetings. Try to attend meetings regularly and make them a priority in your schedule.

Be open-minded: It's important to approach support group meetings with an open mind and a willingness to learn from others. Everyone's experience is different, and you may find that you have something to learn from the experiences of others.

Participate in activities: Many support groups and organizations offer activities and events outside of regular meetings. Participating in these activities can be a great way to build connections with other survivors and help you feel more comfortable in the group.

Speak up when you need help: It's okay to ask for help when you need it. If you're struggling, don't be afraid to speak up and ask for support from the group facilitator or other members.

Be respectful of others: It's important to remember that everyone in the support group is dealing with their own unique challenges and experiences. Be respectful of others and avoid judgment or criticism.

Keep confidentiality in mind: Confidentiality is essential in support groups, and it's important to respect the privacy of other group members. Avoid discussing what other members share outside of the group.

Take advantage of resources: Many local support groups and organizations offer additional resources and services, such as counseling or legal assistance. Take advantage of these resources to help you in your healing journey.

Be patient with yourself: Healing from domestic violence is a process, and it can take time. Be patient with yourself and allow yourself to feel the emotions that come up along the way.

Overall, connecting with local support groups and organizations can be an incredibly valuable part of your healing journey as a survivor of domestic violence. Don't be afraid to reach out for support and take advantage of the resources available to you in your community.

C. Helpful tips and advice for building a better future

Educate yourself on healthy financial habits

As a survivor of financial abuse, it's important to not only seek out resources and support, but also to educate yourself on healthy financial habits. Financial abuse can leave lasting damage and make it difficult to trust yourself with money. But with the right knowledge and skills, you can take control of your finances and build a secure financial future.

Here are a few tips to help you educate yourself on healthy financial habits:

Start with the basics: If you're new to managing your own finances, it's important to start with the basics. This includes learning about budgeting, saving, and credit. There are many online resources and books available that can help you learn these skills. Don't be afraid to ask for help or seek out a financial counselor if you need additional support.

Learn about financial abuse: Understanding what financial abuse is and how it can manifest is an important step in protecting yourself from future abuse. Look for resources that can help you identify the signs of financial abuse and learn how to protect yourself.

Take a financial literacy class: Many community organizations and financial institutions offer free or low-cost financial literacy classes. These classes can help you learn about topics such as budgeting, saving, investing, and credit. Taking a class can also be a great way to connect with other survivors and build a support network.

Seek out financial counseling: Financial counseling can be a valuable resource for survivors of financial abuse. A financial counselor can help you develop a budget, create a debt management plan, and set financial goals. They can also provide you with support and guidance as you work to build a secure financial future.

Use online resources: There are many online resources available that can help you learn about healthy financial habits. Websites such as The Balance, NerdWallet, and Investopedia offer articles and resources on topics such as budgeting, saving, and investing. You can also find online communities and forums where you can connect with other survivors and share your experiences.

Build a support network: Building a support network of friends, family, and professionals can help you stay on track with your financial goals. This network can provide you with emotional support, as well as practical advice and guidance. Look for local support groups or online communities where you can connect with other survivors and share your experiences.

Practice self-care: Surviving financial abuse can be traumatic and stressful. It's important to practice self-care and take care of yourself as you work to rebuild your financial life. This may include activities such as exercise, meditation, or therapy. Taking care of yourself can help you build resilience and stay focused on your goals.

Educating yourself on healthy financial habits is an important step in recovering from financial abuse and building a secure financial future. It can also help you avoid future financial abuse by giving you the knowledge and skills to recognize and protect yourself from financial abuse. Remember to be patient and kind to yourself as you work to learn these skills and rebuild your financial life. With the right support and resources, you can take control of your finances and create a brighter future for yourself.

Create a safety plan for emergencies

As a survivor of financial abuse, it's important to not only seek out resources and support, but also to create a safety plan for emergencies. A safety plan is a personalized plan that outlines specific steps you can take in order to stay safe in situations of danger or crisis. While it's not always easy to predict when an emergency may arise, having a plan in place can help you feel more prepared and in control.

Here are some tips for creating a safety plan for emergencies:

Identify your support network: Make a list of people you can reach out to in an emergency. This may include family members, friends, neighbors, co-workers, or support groups. It's important to have multiple people you can turn to in case someone is unavailable or unable to help.

Identify safe places: Identify safe places you can go to in an emergency, such as a friend's house, a shelter, or a public place like a library or community center. If you have children, make sure to identify safe places for them as well.

Pack an emergency bag: Pack a bag with essential items you would need in case you need to leave quickly, such as clothing, identification documents, medication, and cash. Keep the bag in a safe and accessible place, such as with a trusted friend or in a secure storage unit.

Plan your escape: If you need to leave a dangerous situation, plan your escape ahead of time. Identify the safest and most direct route out of your home or workplace, and practice escaping through that route. Make sure to have a backup plan in case the first route is blocked or unsafe.

Develop a code word: Develop a code word with your support network that indicates you are in danger and need help. Make sure everyone knows the code word and what it means.

Create a list of emergency phone numbers: Make a list of emergency phone numbers, such as 911, your local police department, and your local domestic violence hotline. Keep the list in a safe and accessible place, such as in your emergency bag or with a trusted friend.

Take steps to protect your finances: Financial abuse often goes hand-in-hand with other forms of abuse, and it's important to take steps to protect your finances in case of an emergency. This may include opening a separate bank account, changing your passwords and PIN numbers, and securing important financial documents.

Remember, creating a safety plan is a personal and individual process, and it's important to tailor your plan to your specific situation and needs. If you need help creating a safety plan or accessing resources, don't hesitate to reach out to local support groups or organizations for assistance.

Develop a budget and financial plan

Developing a budget and financial plan is a critical step in regaining control of your financial situation as a survivor of domestic abuse. It can help you establish a sense of financial stability, reduce stress and anxiety, and create a path towards your long-term financial goals. In this chapter, we'll discuss some tips for creating a budget and financial plan that works for you.

Assess your current financial situation
The first step in creating a budget and financial plan is to assess your current financial situation. This includes taking a look at your income, expenses, debts, and assets. Start by gathering all of your financial documents, such as bank statements, credit card bills, and pay stubs. Once you have a clear understanding of your current financial situation, you can start to develop a plan for how to move forward.

Determine your income

The next step is to determine your income. This includes any income you receive from work, as well as any other sources of income, such as child support or government benefits. Make sure to account for any fluctuations in your income, such as seasonal work or variable pay.

Identify your expenses

Once you have a clear understanding of your income, you can start to identify your expenses. Make a list of all of your monthly expenses, including rent or mortgage payments, utilities, groceries, transportation, and any other regular expenses. It's also important to account for any irregular expenses, such as medical bills or car repairs.

Prioritize your expenses

Once you have identified your expenses, it's important to prioritize them based on their importance and urgency. For example, paying your rent or mortgage should be a top priority, while discretionary expenses such as entertainment or dining out may be lower on the list. Make sure to account for any debts you have, such as credit card bills or loans.

Set financial goals

In addition to prioritizing your expenses, it's important to set financial goals for yourself. This could include paying off debt, building up an emergency fund, or saving for a long-term goal such as buying a home or starting a business. Make sure your goals are specific, measurable, achievable, relevant, and time-bound.

Create a budget

Once you have assessed your current financial situation, determined your income, identified your expenses, prioritized your expenses, and set financial goals, you can start to create a budget. A budget is a plan for how you will allocate your income towards your expenses and financial goals. Make sure to account for any irregular expenses and unexpected emergencies.

Monitor and adjust your budget

Creating a budget is just the first step. It's important to monitor your budget regularly and make adjustments as needed. This could include cutting back on discretionary expenses, finding ways to increase your income, or re-prioritizing your expenses based on changes in your financial situation.

Seek help if needed

Creating a budget and financial plan can be a challenging process, especially if you have experienced financial abuse. Don't hesitate to seek help from a financial advisor or counselor, or from organizations that specialize in supporting survivors of domestic abuse. They can provide you with guidance and support as you work towards your financial goals.

In conclusion, creating a budget and financial plan is an important step in regaining control of your finances and building a stable, secure future. By assessing your current financial situation, identifying your income and expenses, setting financial goals, and creating a budget, you can take control of your finances and work towards achieving your long-term financial goals. Remember to monitor your budget regularly and seek help if needed, and don't hesitate to celebrate your progress along the way.

Build a support network

Building a support network is an essential part of the healing process for survivors of domestic violence. A support network can provide emotional support, practical assistance, and a sense of community. It's important to remember that you are not alone and that there are people and resources available to help you.

Here are some tips to help you build a support network:

Identify your needs: Take some time to identify what kind of support you need. Do you need someone to talk to, help with childcare, or assistance finding a job? Once you have a clear understanding of your needs, you can start to look for people and resources that can provide the support you need.

Reach out to friends and family: Friends and family members can be a great source of support. Let them know what you're going through and what kind of support you need. If you don't feel comfortable talking to someone you know, consider reaching out to a support group or a domestic violence hotline.

Join a support group: Support groups can be a great way to connect with other survivors and find emotional support. Look for local support groups or online forums where you can connect with others who have gone through similar experiences.

Connect with community resources: There are many community resources available to survivors of domestic violence, including shelters, legal aid clinics, and counseling services. These resources can provide practical support and help you build a strong support network.

Consider therapy: Therapy can be a helpful way to process your experiences and develop coping skills. A therapist can also help you identify and address any negative patterns or beliefs that may be impacting your ability to build a support network.

Be patient: Building a support network takes time and effort. Don't get discouraged if it takes a while to find the right people and resources. Keep reaching out and trying new things until you find a support network that works for you.

Practice self-care: Taking care of yourself is an important part of building a support network. Make sure to prioritize self-care activities, such as exercise, meditation, or spending time with friends, as part of your overall support network plan.

Remember, building a support network is not a one-time event. It's an ongoing process that requires effort and commitment. But with the right resources and mindset, you can create a strong and supportive network that will help you heal and thrive.

Prioritize self-care and healing

As a survivor of domestic violence, it's important to prioritize self-care and healing in your journey towards recovery. It's not easy to overcome the trauma of abuse, but with the right support and tools, it is possible to heal and move forward.

Here are some tips to help you prioritize self-care and healing:

Seek professional help: Seeking help from a therapist or counselor can be a valuable resource in the healing process. A trained professional can help you process your experiences, develop coping skills, and work through any lingering trauma. Look for a therapist who specializes in trauma or domestic violence and who you feel comfortable with.

Practice self-compassion: Be kind to yourself and acknowledge that healing is a journey, not a destination. Give yourself permission to take breaks when you need them and practice self-care regularly. This could mean taking a walk, practicing mindfulness, or treating yourself to something you enjoy.

Connect with others: Building a support network of people who understand your experiences and can offer you emotional support can be invaluable in the healing process. This can include friends, family members, support groups, or online communities. Reach out to those who have been there before and can offer you guidance and understanding.

Engage in activities that bring you joy: Domestic violence can leave you feeling depleted and disconnected from the things that used to bring you joy. It's important to make time for activities that make you happy, whether it's painting, cooking, dancing, or anything else. Engaging in activities that bring you joy can help boost your mood and improve your overall well-being.

Set boundaries: Setting boundaries is an important aspect of self-care, especially after experiencing domestic violence. This can include setting limits on your time and energy, saying "no" to things that don't serve you, and establishing clear boundaries with others. Prioritizing your needs and setting boundaries can help you feel more in control of your life and reduce feelings of overwhelm and stress.

Practice forgiveness: Forgiving yourself and others can be a powerful tool in the healing process. Forgiveness doesn't mean forgetting what happened or excusing abusive behavior, but it does mean letting go of resentment and anger. This can be a difficult process, but it can help you move forward and let go of the negative emotions that may be holding you back.

Take care of your physical health: Domestic violence can take a toll on your physical health as well as your emotional well-being. It's important to take care of your physical health by eating well, exercising, and getting enough sleep. This can help you feel more energized and better equipped to handle the challenges of healing from abuse.

Set achievable goals: Setting achievable goals can help you build momentum and feel a sense of accomplishment. These goals could be as simple as taking a walk every day or attending a support group meeting once a week. Start small and build from there.

Remember, healing from domestic violence is a process that takes time and effort. But with the right support and tools, you can overcome the trauma and move forward towards a brighter future. Prioritizing self-care and healing is an important part of this journey, and it's never too late to start.

Set goals for your future and work towards them

As a survivor of domestic violence, it can be difficult to imagine a future beyond the trauma and pain of abuse. However, setting goals and working towards them can help you reclaim your sense of agency and purpose. Here are some tips to help you set and achieve your goals:

Start with small, achievable goals: When setting goals, it's important to start with small, achievable steps. This can help you build momentum and confidence as you work towards bigger goals. For example, you could set a goal to attend a support group or reach out to a friend for emotional support.

Identify your values and priorities: Your goals should be aligned with your values and priorities. Take some time to reflect on what matters most to you, and use that as a guide when setting goals. For example, if family is important to you, you might set a goal to rebuild relationships with family members after the trauma of abuse.

Make your goals SMART: SMART stands for Specific, Measurable, Achievable, Relevant, and Time-bound. When setting goals, make sure they meet these criteria. For example, instead of setting a vague goal to "get healthier," you might set a SMART goal to walk for 30 minutes three times a week.

Break down bigger goals into smaller steps: If you have a big goal, like going back to school or starting a new career, it can be helpful to break it down into smaller, manageable steps. For example, you might start by researching schools or job opportunities, then creating a resume or application, and finally attending interviews or enrolling in classes.

Celebrate your progress: It's important to celebrate your progress along the way, even if you haven't achieved your ultimate goal yet. Take time to acknowledge your hard work and accomplishments, and use that as motivation to keep going.

Be flexible: Life can be unpredictable, and sometimes circumstances change. It's important to be flexible and adjust your goals as needed. This doesn't mean giving up on your goals altogether, but rather finding new ways to achieve them that are better suited to your current situation.

Seek support: Achieving goals can be challenging, and it's important to have a support system in place. Reach out to friends, family, or a therapist for support and encouragement as you work towards your goals.

By setting and working towards goals, you can reclaim your sense of agency and purpose after the trauma of abuse. Remember to start small, identify your values and priorities, make your goals SMART, break down bigger goals into smaller steps, celebrate your progress, be flexible, and seek support along the way.

Seek out additional resources and support as needed

As a survivor of domestic violence, it is important to remember that healing is a journey, and you do not have to go through it alone. There are many resources and support systems available to help you along the way. In this chapter, we will discuss the importance of seeking out additional resources and support as needed.

One of the most important things to keep in mind as a survivor is that healing is a process, and it takes time. There may be times when you feel overwhelmed or unsure of how to move forward. This is normal, and it is important to reach out for help when you need it.

There are many resources available to survivors of domestic violence, including hotlines, support groups, counseling services, and legal assistance. These resources can help you navigate the challenges you may face, and provide you with the tools and support you need to move forward.

National and Local Hotlines: The National Domestic Violence Hotline and many local hotlines are available 24/7 to provide support and assistance to survivors. They can provide you with information about resources in your area, safety planning, and emotional support.

Support Groups: Joining a support group can be a great way to connect with other survivors and share your experiences. It can be a safe and supportive environment where you can discuss your feelings and get advice from others who have been through similar experiences.

Counseling Services: Counseling can be a powerful tool in the healing process. It can provide you with a safe and supportive environment to explore your feelings and work through the trauma you have experienced. There are many different types of counseling available, including individual therapy, group therapy, and online counseling.

Legal Assistance: Legal assistance can be crucial for survivors who are seeking protection orders or navigating the legal system. There are many organizations that provide free or low-cost legal assistance to survivors, including legal aid societies, domestic violence clinics, and pro bono attorneys.

Financial Assistance: Financial abuse is a common tactic used by abusers, and many survivors may need financial assistance to help them get back on their feet. There are many organizations that provide financial assistance to survivors, including job training programs, housing assistance programs, and emergency financial assistance programs.

In addition to these resources, it is also important to seek out the support of family and friends. Building a strong support network can provide you with emotional support, encouragement, and a sense of community. It is important to surround yourself with people who love and care about you, and who will support you as you work towards healing and recovery.

Remember, healing is a journey, and it is important to be patient and kind to yourself. It is okay to seek out additional resources and support as needed, and to take things one step at a time. With the right tools and support, you can overcome the trauma of domestic violence and build a brighter future for yourself.

In conclusion, seeking support and resources is crucial for survivors of financial abuse to regain control of their finances and lives. Whether it's reaching out to a local support group, developing a budget and financial plan, or prioritizing self-care and healing, survivors can take steps towards a brighter future. It's important to remember that healing and recovery take time and that each survivor's journey is unique. By being patient, seeking out resources and support as needed, and staying committed to their goals, survivors can create a path towards financial stability and overall well-being.

CHAPTER 7 CONCLUSION

❖ Final thoughts on healing from financial abuse
❖ Encouragement for the reader
❖ Hope for a brighter future

Congratulations on reaching the end of this guide. By reading through each chapter, you have taken an important step towards healing from financial abuse and reclaiming your financial independence. We hope that this guide has been helpful and provided you with the knowledge, tools, and resources you need to move forward.

As a survivor of financial abuse, it can be challenging to navigate the complexities of rebuilding your financial life. But, it's important to remember that you are not alone. There are many others who have been through similar experiences and have found ways to overcome financial abuse and move towards a brighter future.

In this final chapter, we would like to offer some words of encouragement and hope. We understand that the healing journey is not easy, and there may be times when it feels overwhelming. But, we want to remind you that it is possible to heal from financial abuse and create a life that is full of abundance and financial stability.

Through the chapters of this guide, we have covered a variety of topics, including understanding financial abuse, developing a budget and financial plan, building a support network, and setting goals for the future. By applying the principles discussed in this guide, you can take meaningful steps towards financial healing.

Remember to be patient and kind to yourself during this process. Healing from financial abuse is a journey, and it may take time. But, with the right resources, support, and mindset, you can overcome financial abuse and create a life that is filled with financial security, joy, and abundance.

We encourage you to continue seeking out additional resources and support as needed. The journey towards financial healing is not one that you have to take alone. There are many organizations and support groups available to help you along the way.

In closing, we would like to thank you for taking the time to read this guide. We hope that it has been a valuable resource for you on your journey towards healing from financial abuse. Remember, you are strong, capable, and worthy of a life free from financial abuse. We wish you all the best as you continue on your healing journey.

Final thoughts on healing from financial abuse

As a survivor of financial abuse, I know firsthand the devastating impact it can have on every aspect of your life. It can be a long and difficult journey to heal from the trauma and regain control of your finances, but it is possible. In this final chapter, I want to offer some encouragement and final thoughts on the healing process.

First and foremost, it's important to remember that healing from financial abuse is not a linear process. There will be good days and bad days, progress and setbacks. It's important to be patient with yourself and to celebrate even the smallest victories along the way.

One of the most important steps in healing from financial abuse is to address the trauma that has been inflicted upon you. This may involve seeking therapy or counseling from a qualified professional who specializes in trauma and domestic violence. It can be difficult to confront the pain and trauma that you have experienced, but it is necessary in order to move forward.

In addition to seeking professional help, building a support network can be incredibly beneficial in the healing process. Surround yourself with people who believe in you, who will support you through the ups and downs, and who will encourage you to keep moving forward. This may include family and friends, as well as local support groups and organizations.

It's also important to prioritize self-care as part of the healing process. This may involve engaging in activities that bring you joy and fulfillment, such as exercise, meditation, or spending time in nature. It may also involve setting boundaries and saying no to things that are not serving your overall well-being.

As you begin to regain control of your finances, it can be helpful to set specific goals for your future and work towards them. This may involve creating a budget and financial plan, as well as seeking out additional resources and support as needed. It's important to remember that financial stability is a process, and it's okay to ask for help along the way.

Finally, I want to offer some words of encouragement and hope for a brighter future. It's easy to feel overwhelmed and discouraged when you are in the midst of healing from financial abuse, but know that there is a light at the end of the tunnel. With patience, perseverance, and a commitment to your own well-being, you can overcome the trauma of financial abuse and build a brighter future for yourself.

Remember that you are not alone, and there are resources and support available to you. Whether you are just beginning your healing journey or are well on your way, know that there is hope for a brighter future. Keep pushing forward, and know that you are capable of overcoming the challenges that come your way.

Encouragement for the reader

As a survivor of financial abuse, I want to take a moment to encourage you on your journey towards healing and recovery. I know firsthand how difficult and overwhelming it can be to navigate the aftermath of financial abuse, but I also know that it is possible to overcome and move forward towards a brighter future.

First and foremost, I want you to know that you are not alone. There are countless individuals who have experienced financial abuse and have found a way to rebuild their lives. You are strong and capable of overcoming this challenge.

It's important to acknowledge that healing is a process, and there will be ups and downs along the way. It's okay to take things one day at a time and to seek out support when you need it. Remember, healing is not a linear process, and it's okay if you have setbacks or moments of struggle. What's important is that you continue to move forward and work towards your goals.

I also want to remind you to be kind to yourself. It's easy to blame yourself for the abuse or to feel like you should have seen the signs earlier. But the reality is that financial abuse is a form of control, and it's not your fault. You deserve love, respect, and financial stability, and there is no shame in seeking out resources and support to help you achieve these things.

As you move forward, I encourage you to set realistic goals for yourself. This could be as simple as creating a budget, finding a new job, or working towards financial independence. Whatever your goals may be, remember that they are achievable with hard work and dedication.

It's also important to prioritize self-care and take time to nurture your mental, emotional, and physical well-being. This could mean seeking out therapy or counseling, engaging in activities that bring you joy, or connecting with supportive friends and family members.

Remember that healing is a journey, and it's okay to take the time you need to focus on yourself and your well-being. You are worthy of love, respect, and financial stability, and you have the strength and resilience to overcome the challenges you face.

Finally, I want to leave you with a message of hope. Healing from financial abuse is possible, and there is a brighter future waiting for you on the other side. It may not be easy, but with the right resources and support, you can overcome this challenge and build a life of financial stability, security, and independence.

I believe in you, and I know that you have what it takes to create a brighter future for yourself. Keep pushing forward, and remember that you are not alone.

Hope for a brighter future

As a survivor of financial abuse, it may feel like your world has been turned upside down. You may be struggling to make ends meet, dealing with debt, and trying to rebuild your life. It's important to remember that healing is a journey, and there is hope for a brighter future.

First and foremost, it's important to recognize the strength and resilience that brought you this far. Surviving financial abuse takes incredible strength and courage, and it's important to give yourself credit for what you've overcome. No matter how challenging the road ahead may seem, remember that you are capable of facing it head-on.

It's also important to remember that healing is a process, and it's okay to take your time. There may be setbacks and obstacles along the way, but with support and perseverance, you can overcome them. Don't be afraid to reach out for help when you need it, whether that means seeking therapy or connecting with support groups.

As you work towards healing from financial abuse, it's important to set goals for yourself and work towards them. These goals may be financial, such as paying off debt or building a savings account, or they may be personal, such as pursuing a new career or hobby. Whatever your goals may be, remember that they are within your reach and that you have the strength and determination to achieve them.

Remember that self-care is crucial to your healing journey. This may mean taking time for yourself to engage in activities that bring you joy and peace, or it may mean seeking professional help to work through trauma and other emotional challenges. Taking care of yourself will help you build resilience and strengthen your ability to face challenges.

Finally, it's important to hold onto hope for a brighter future. Healing from financial abuse is a journey, but it is also a journey towards a life that is free from abuse and full of possibility. With each step you take towards healing, you are creating a brighter future for yourself.

In conclusion, as you continue on your healing journey, remember to celebrate your strength and resilience, take your time, set goals, prioritize self-care, and hold onto hope. The road may be challenging at times, but with the right support and mindset, you can create a brighter future for yourself.